AF260870

RIDING ON MERLIN'S BROOM

Sketches from the Life of a Vagabond Kid

By Jim Gage

*. . .all that has passed on before appear to me
as vanished shadows, too far away to grasp
the details, yet clear enough to allow
imagination to supply the perspective.*

Edgar Rye, *The Quirt and the Spur*, 1909.

RIDING ON MERLIN'S BROOM: Sketches from the Life of a Vagabond Kid
Copyright © 2014 by Jim Gage
ISBN-13: 978-1496115904
ISBN-10: 1496115902

Excerpt from A SAND COUNTY ALMANAC by Aldo Leopold
© 1949 by Oxford University Press, Inc.

Published by:
 Jim Gage for JAG Productions, Aztec, NM

Printed in the United States of America. All rights reserved under International Copyright Law. Contents may not be reproduced in whole or in part in any way without the express written consent of the publisher. For information, contact Jim Gage, 50 C.R. 2101, Aztec, NM 87410

JAG Productions

To Mark

The best of us

Too soon gone.

*Without ties to our ancestors,
we are lonely specks of dust,
adrift and floating, attached to
nothing and no one.*

Tess Gerritsen, *The Silent Girl*

*Whatever you do will be
insignificant and it is very
important that you do it.*

Mohandas Gandhi

1.

<u>Winter 2002</u>

Before dawn on this frosty, last day of February, I pack our little red Capri convertible with possibles and set out for Denton, 800 miles away. A mug of hot coffee is in the holder, hat and gloves on to ward off the early morning chill. The thermometer outside our bedroom window read 10 degrees at 6 AM.

From this perch on the northwestern edge of New Mexico, I will angle southeast to Albuquerque, then a left turn onto I-40 across New Mexico and the Texas Panhandle to the cross timbers country of North Texas, where I spent most of my growing-up years. On this week-long odyssey I hope to refresh some of the stale memories of those times, to fill in some of the gaps of remembrance that have been eroded by the passing years.

My mission: to collect and validate as much as I can from those who are still here, then compare it with what I think I know, to come up with sketches of my life that may be of interest to my children and grandchildren. Looking back through that tunnel of time, I see bits and pieces of long-ago events. After the passage of several decades, I'm not even sure they are my memories; they may be recollections of times I have heard my mom and a few others talk about. Over the years I have made numerous random entries in my journals regarding childhood memories and family members' recollections which have recently been ordered into a rough draft. Now that age is taking my family, it is time to get serious about chronicling this part of my family history if it is to be preserved at all.

Hope it's not too late. My mother, at 92, suffers from both short- and long-term memory problems. All her siblings are gone or beyond recalling, and my father's two remaining sisters are in their 80s. I am hoping my aunts living in Wise County can help with some of the details of our life in the late 1930s and early 40s which I was too young to remember. It's Now or Never Time, so I'm taking this week to try to get on paper, and more clearly fixed in my memory, the details of those early years that are too fuzzy, vague or simply forgotten.

I have been piddlin' around with this notion for several years: to write about some remembered childhood adventures in some of the places our family lived during my early years. We moved around a lot, eight or nine times by the time I was twelve years old. What affect did those vagabond years have on me? Did those wanderings imprint on me a wanderlust that kept me on the move for much of my adult life? Perhaps by the time this journey is over, I'll have some insights.

The trek from Northwest New Mexico to Denton, made many times, takes about thirteen hours, with stops only for gas and to "drain my radiator." The drive seems to get harder each time I make it, like so many things have become now that I have officially reached senior citizen status. This time out, the trip is brutal.

By the time I cross the state border into Texas, about halfway there, my back hurts and my bladder has needed emptying more often than usual. In Adrian, just west of Amarillo, I pull off I-40 for gas and a much needed pit stop, trying to hurry, but creaky and stiff-legged from the long drive, move crab-like toward the mom and pop station. Even the stiff northwest wind at my back doesn't help move me along fast enough. My bladder control is not what it once was and I feel a wet trickle down my leg as I open the door into the station and scurry to the Men's Room, hoping the lady behind the counter doesn't look too closely.

But what a relief this one is, even with the dribble. Ahhh! The pause that refreshes!

As I exit the warm station, the whistling wind instantly chills me where the wet spot is. Scurrying to the warmth of the car, I wonder how often this scenario is repeated by weak-bladdered geezers like me. How many times a day do gas station attendants witness this piss-in-the-pants shuffle—graying guys holding their caps or hats at half- mast upon entering or exiting the john of a gas station? Is this the reason so many men my age wear some kind of head gear, not as cover from the sun as we might believe, but to hide the dribble? Maybe I should do a survey, figure the percentages, calculate the odds. Is it one out of three; as high as 50%? Here's a research study I'll bet no one has done yet. Maybe the folks who produce Saw Palmetto and other aids to bladder control would fund it. I'm a pretty good grant writer, maybe I could get one.

Several hours later, I wheel into the familiar driveway on Alice Street in Denton. It is dark now and I am both exhausted and wired from the trip, like a football player after winning a big game. My daughter Dana has a delicious meal of cabbage and sausages cooking on the stove. It is good to be back in the home of my youth. This night, I sleep better than I have in days. Plagued by a sleep disorder for years, it is refreshing to have a good night's sleep for a change.

The next day is Friday, and I spend most of the morning recuperating from the previous day's long drive before visiting with my mom in the nursing home. It is as I feared; she cannot recall much regarding some specific questions I have prepared about those early years. I leave the questions with her to think about, to try to recall forgotten details. Later, I have a long-overdue talk with my brother, Jerry, who is four-and-a-half years my junior. Although we are close we rarely talk on the phone, choosing face-to-face chatter when I come for a visit. We get caught up on family happenings, then spend a couple of hours reminiscing about some of the early days. He knows about my writing project, has been encouraging me for years to get on with it. Now that I am, he is an ardent supporter. We have some good laughs about some of the long-ago adventures we had, him recalling some details I had forgotten.

"Be sure you put that one in," he says on more than one occasion as a particular hi-jinx is retold. It is interesting to hear his spin on things, how he remembers incidents I had forgotten, to see those times from his perspective. It is feeling more like a family project, and I'm beginning to wonder, not for the first time, how all this information will get filtered into a readable final product—one that is not as deadly boring as watching someone else's vacation slides. This is going to be trickier than I thought.

Later, Dana and I go over to an old friend's house for an evening of drinks, dinner and friendly chatter. I have known Ann Reeves Houston since high school, and as friends who have seen each other through divorce, children, grandchildren, aging and dying parents—there is very little we cannot share.

Several years ago, single again, Ann changed careers, moved back to Denton and became a successful real estate broker. We talk about our families, our high school and college days, about Texas politics, in the familiar way of old friends. I am reminded how much leaving this town I grew up in, how living and working in several states has changed my outlook since moving away after college graduation. This is a topic Ann and I have explored more than once over the years—how our moving about has changed our world view.

As I have returned to Denton over the years for visits, family gatherings, and high school reunions, I have come to realize the importance of *place* in my life. Someone once said, "Geography is destiny." I know geography is a major player in my life story. My ties here are no longer strong. I am anchored farther west now, on the edge of New Mexico on a few acres overlooking the Animas River. But in a larger sense, I am rooted in numerous places throughout the West— in Oregon, Montana, Colorado and the Big Bend Country of West Texas. And in Mexico, now that my son Blake and his wife Pam are permanent residents there in Baja. I am a citizen of the West, and love all the places where I have lived. Susan and I are blessed to have this little secluded chunk of "God's Country," my perfect place, where I expect live out the remainder of my days.

My vagabond, rolling stone nature has knocked off a lot of the mossy provincialism that seems to grow when one remains in the same spot for a long time. Sometimes I allow my egocentrism to have the upper hand as I note the contrast with my school chums who have remained rooted to this area of Texas, but these are just differences which time and life experiences have wrought. Education and experience don't make us more alike, they make us more different. I was much more like my classmates when we were high school seniors than I am now that we are senior citizens. Except for those I have remained in contact with through the years, sharing our life's experiences like I have with Ann and a few others, today we have little in common except having shared some youthful experiences a half-century ago.

Nona Belle Reding - 1933

2.

"We put on a wedding, and nobody came."

My mom says this the following morning, along with a nudge and a shy, sad smile. We sit in her room at the Good Samaritan Retirement Center in Denton, talking about some precious, fading memories. As the oldest grandchild in my father's family, I have remembrances and experiences of those long-ago times with grandparents none of my younger cousins or my brother have. Knowing there may not be much time left, I scribble furiously in my journal as Mom talks about her wedding day and early times with my dad. This is the story I cobbled together over several years, gleaned from Mom's recollections and many of my own, kept for years in personal journals, and some from a few family members whom I have overheard at earlier times.

Three days after Christmas, 1933, Jim George Gage and Nona Belle Reding were married in the home of the Methodist minister in Decatur, Texas. It was a cold, snowy day in the depths of the Great Depression. They had planned to get married on Christmas Day, but an early winter storm on Christmas Eve howled down from Canada across that cross timbers section of North Texas, rendering the roads icy, snow-packed and impassable. Wedding guests were unable to travel, and the postponed ceremony that day was attended only by the minister, his wife, and my mother's best friend, Evelyn Washburn. JG and Nona drove to Ft. Worth to spend their wedding night in the home of her sister, Beula Loter.

After a weekend honeymoon, they returned to rural Wise County to begin their life together in the home of paternal grandparents. This was the first of many dwellings they were to share during their vagabond, hard-scrabble life of the next fifteen years. In 1954, the year I graduated from Denton High School, they bought their second and final home, a modest three-bedroom they were to live in together for the next 43 years.

In my father's family, long marriages are the norm. When Dad's youngest sister, Merlyne, and her husband Warren Hunt celebrated their 50th wedding anniversary in 1996, a family photo of all five Gage brothers, sisters and spouses capture a memorable moment—these five brothers and sisters had all been married at least 50 years. At the time of my father's death in 1997, JG and Nona Gage had been married for 64 years.

Nona and JG

Nona was the fourth of six children born to Caleb and Jennie Reding on April 14, 1910. All of the Reding children were born at home on the family farm, a parcel of land carved from the larger section farmed by Caleb's father until his death, then divided among the siblings. The farm was located a few miles south of Slidell in Northeast Wise County.

In later years Nona mentioned the "bad blood" that existed between Caleb and his two sisters over the way the family farm was divided after the death of her grandfather. No details are known about this family feud, other than one of the parcels was sold soon after the inheritance. One sister retained her adjacent parcel, which Caleb also farmed until it, too, was sold years later. By the time I came along the farm had been sold and Mama and Papa were now farming the Ray Foreman place in southeast Denton County. My fox hunting times with Papa were in this part of the county, which was then a cross-timbered swatch interspersed with small and medium-sized farms.

Farming in that area of north central Texas was a chancy thing in the 1920s and 30s. It was chancy throughout the Southwest—think being on the southern edge of the Dust Bowl. Average rainfall was 25–30 inches during most years, but these were *bad* years, with most during this time period averaging less than fifteen inches. Dry land farming suffered during these years, and if your farming operation was small and marginal, as the Reding farm was, as were many others, the times were very lean.

Parched land yields scant crops—it is almost impossible to grown grain or animal feed on less than twenty inches of rainfall per year, particularly if the rain falls at inopportune times. No irrigated fields in those days.

It was during these bleak times of too-little rainfall and economic hardship that Nona and JG grew into adulthood and began their life together.

A pause as I write this, pick up a photo taken of Nona sometime before her wedding in 1933. A shy smile, dark eyes stare back at me; brunette hair, shiny-black in this black-and-white shot, wavy, '20's stylish hair completes this picture. She was a tall, striking beauty, at 5' 8" the same height as my father. All who knew Nona in her youth said she was popular, a good student at Slidell High School, a basketball player who was faster than most of the boys.

She also had a strict, no-nonsense mother who kept a tight rein on her two youngest daughters, Nona and Gladys, after the two oldest, Lela and Beula, sneaked off to marry two guys who turned out to be good-for-nothing drunks. Hubert, the only remaining brother and next-to-the-oldest (a second brother, born after my mom, died a few days after birth), left home at sixteen to cowboy on West Texas ranches. He died of health issues related to alcoholism the year I graduated from High School. Nona and JG were teetotalers their entire lives.

Nona left Slidell High School in 1928 without graduating (she lacked half-a-credit), wanting to be with her class now a year ahead of her in school. She had contracted measles and then pneumonia at the beginning of fourth grade, was gravely ill for a couple of months, missed a lot of school that year. Her mother insisted she repeat this grade—though there was no need to—which put her a year behind her other classmates.

Nona finished high school harboring a secret desire—she wanted to go to college at North Texas in Denton, but had no resources to get there. She *did* have a plan, and only two people knew about it—her younger sister Gladys and her best friend who later served as her Maid of Honor. They wanted to go to college, too.

Her plan was this: Caleb had agreed to allow her to use a small corner of a field, about two acres, to plant some cotton. Cotton was about the only certain cash crop grown in Wise County—hay and grain crops were grown mainly as feed for a farmer's livestock. She would plant, cultivate, care for, pick it when ripe, and get to keep the profit from that cotton for her own use. She asked for no one's assistance, did all the work herself, in addition to whatever other family chores or work that had to be done. Nona labored in that small cotton patch all summer and fall, finally picking it with her mother's help in early

November, driving the cotton wagon to the cotton gin in Krum several miles away. The amount delivered ginned up to a little more than two bales of cotton, 1100 pounds, sold for slightly more than $100.

A year later, the stock market crash of 1929 would make that same cotton sell for less than $25. Many farmers said at that time their cotton was hardly worth picking.

Nona was tired from the back-breaking work, but pleased and excited that she had done it! Her pleasure and excitement was short-lived, however, when at the end of the fall cotton harvest her father gave her $10 and told her the family needed the rest.

I recalled a brief mention of this cotton story at an earlier time, but now hearing a more complete version, with the unrealized dream of going to college in Denton as the clincher, I was stunned. How could he do this to my mother?

"Weren't you angry at Papa?" I asked.

"Yeah, for a while, but I got over it. More sad than angry, I guess," then added with a sliver of a smile, "but it's true, the family *did* need it. Jimmy, I hope you never have to know how hard it was back then. We were barely makin' it, an' if Mama hadn't had a big garden, an' we hadn't had hogs and chickens we would have starved to death. We ate pretty good, but we had no money, hardly anyone did."

Mom talks more about those hard times, how she and others coped. Never a complainer, there was nothing about the frustrations and shattered dreams of a young woman with few options: "I did get to go to North Texas, years later, but it was to work at Chilton Hall as a cook in the cafeteria." This with another smile and a knowing nudge to my leg. I remembered her first job in Denton after we moved there in 1948.

"That was a main reason we wanted to move to Denton. JG and I wanted you and Jerry to be able to go to college, and about the only way was for us to move here." Unspoken was another reason, one pieced together from snippets of conversations overheard between Mom and Dad over the years: A few months before we left the farm for the town life of Denton, Dad had sustained a farm injury, a severed little finger of his left hand from the operation of a hedge trimmer.

Around a farm or ranch, where machinery operation and the working of cattle and horses make injuries fairly common, it is rare for anyone to escape unscathed. A few years earlier, Mom had broken a finger while swinging around a wire fence, barely eluding the horns of a momma cow enraged by the penning up of her calf. I had been thrown or fallen off of numerous horses and a few calves with no notable injuries, but my uncle Hubert, the only real cowboy in my family, had had two broken legs, a fractured pelvis and ruptured spinal disc during his rodeo and horse-wrangling years. I had heard that my grandfather Merlin had been kicked by a mule and had his spleen removed, perhaps the first of several operations which led to his early death.

This was my dad's final farm injury, but many years earlier a malady of another sort occurred which changed his life forever. In August, a week from his sixteenth birthday, JG was helping bail hay on the Gage family farm. The heat was scorching, and in the middle of the afternoon, the hottest part of the day with no breeze, in a hay field down near Denton Creek he kept working after he got too hot to continue, passed out, suffered a heat stroke. When found a few minutes later, he was unconscious. He was taken to the shade to cool off, but it was too late.

He remained in a coma for three days, and almost died.

Dad's younger sister, Roberta, was a water-carrier for the haying crew that day: "I saw him on the ground, ran over to help him up, but he was so still and white as a sheet. I thought he was dead. We finally carried him to the house, Momma tried to cool him off. The doctor finally came from Decatur, and he said it was serious."

Three days later he slowly came out of his coma, and from here the story gets vague and unclear. Gage family members provide different versions of what happened, but the bottom line is that Dad's mental, visual and speech abilities were dramatically altered. It took weeks for him to regain his speech and vision. He could no longer read or write. When school began in September, he would have been a junior at Slidell High School, but JG never returned to school.

Instead, after a slow recovery, for the next six years his experience and skills were devoted primarily to raising and showing beef cattle—he already knew how to farm and work dairy cattle, since there were always several cows to milk and care for. Dad had been milking cows daily since he was six years old, and I never heard him complain about having to start this grind so young, or about how hard his father was on him, the oldest child.

For a couple of years Dad was "farmed out" to a cousin, Dr. Joe Allen, who had a ranch near Justin. JG assisted with the livestock and lived at the Allen place. This was the same Joe Allen who delivered me.

Later he went to Arlington Junior College where he worked at the Ag Program with dairy and beef cattle. Early on, we had been led to believe that Dad *went* to Arlington JC. Yeah, he *went* there to *work*, not go to school as we thought; a little obfuscation only cleared up decades later, after he was gone.

It was my mom who gave only the briefest of explanations of Dad's life during this time before they met and married: "Your grandfather Merlin was a hard man, stern, a hard-worker. He expected his kids to work hard right along-side him, but only JG and Roberta did. Ralph (a year younger) hated farm work, left home soon as he could for college. Lavada did too, and Merlyne was too little."

She later adds: "I reckon Merlin tried to do too much without enough help, an' his health finally gave out. Your daddy could never do enough to please him, but he sure tried."

I never really got to know or spend much time with my Grandfather Merlin. There is only one fond, gentle memory: One summer when I was four or five he took me swimming with him in the spring-fed pond where the family got most of its drinking water. He was probably recovering from his latest operation, but feeling well enough to swim, with me on his back, in the small spring about 100 yards from the house, down closer to Denton Creek. I remember the cool, clear water on a hot summer day, the spring shaded by oak, hickory and persimmon trees all around. It was a special moment in time; I never got another one.

That was it. Three years later he was gone at age 53.

Merlin

Merlin Monroe Gage was one of four brothers, tall look-alikes who settled on adjacent bottom-land farms along Denton Creek after earning most of the money to pay for their land by working for a coal-mining outfit near Trinidad, Colorado. Knowing now something of the violent history which erupted in that area of Southern Colorado a couple of years later when unions were just being formed, I have wondered what horrid working conditions these Gages had to endure.

Did they ever talk much about the hardships of those mining years, of how lucky they were to avoid the miner's strikes and the bloodbath which followed?

A few years into the 20th Century, the Industrial Revolution in full swing, working conditions in many industrial sites were abysmal—this was particularly true in the coal-mining industry where mine safety regulations were an afterthought. The mines in the Trinidad area were reputed to be the worst, leading the nation in mining deaths for several years. These four brothers were on-the-ground witnesses to the beginning of unionization and the inhuman treatment of mine workers. Soon after they returned to Texas over a hundred miners were shot down during the mine riots that got so out of hand the Governor of Colorado had to call out the state militia.

Did these young men witness the beginnings of violence which later swelled to an avalanche? No family member knows anything of the personal side of this story, though Hollywood has given us some generic versions. I have often wished to have the information needed to tell this unknown segment of Gage family history.

Three of the brothers returned to Texas and settled in the same vicinity of Wise County; the fourth went to California. After mining in Colorado for a couple of years, Merlin rode the train from Trinidad to Missouri to get my grandmother, Buena Griffith, and married her there;

Merlin and Buena Gage on their wedding day

they then came back to Texas and began their life together on the Gage family farm near Decatur. My father was born at home on August 27, 1911, the first of five children my grandparents would have.

There are so many things parents never tell their children. I did not know any of this about my father or grandfather as I was growing up. Years later, as I began asking questions about Gage and Reding family histories, some of the blank spaces slowly filled, but there are still blank spaces I want to know about. Too late now, there is only speculation and guesswork.

A memory from my high school years takes on a different meaning after knowing some of this history. On a few occasions, as I came home at night from an excursion, entering the kitchen from the back door as always, Mom and Dad sat at the kitchen table, papers and a book or two are scattered around. Seeing me there was a rustle to put these things away, but I gave it little attention, probably tired and eager for bed. It is only much later, after some prodding of Mom who reluctantly and briefly tells a little about this. What was I interrupting? It was a lesson from Mom—she was helping Dad with his reading and writing!

When we moved to Denton, Dad went to work for Moore Business Forms, Inc., a large international paper company, working for 25 years in the Stock Department until he retired. After a few years he was offered a foreman's job, and after a couple of refusals, finally took the supervisory position. His refusals of the advancement were because he thought he could not read or write well enough to do the paperwork. It was only after Mom's help with his reading and writing, and often bringing paperwork home so she could help him with it, that he took the foreman's job.

This helps explain something else I noticed but did not tune in to—how Dad seemed to labor over reading the newspaper, and always preferred to *watch and hear* the news as delivered on TV. Duh, come in world! How clueless can one kid be?

We all have secret lives. Since learning of these hidden truths and hardships I have come to more deeply admire and appreciate who my parents were and how they came to be. The struggles endured, the heart-breaking setbacks overcome awe me to this day.

3.

The next day I plan to begin the trek to Decatur, Northeastern Wise County and back into the past, but the weather doesn't cooperate. Seems I brought winter weather with me—rain, snow and sleet most of the day, keeping us inside.

I use the time to do some writing, and to read a book of essays about the new West, *Kill the Cowboy*, by Sharman Apt Russell. Her balanced reporting of the struggles and conflicts between western environmentalists and ranchers strike an agreeable chord; some notes for future reference are made. Her accounts of trappers and wolf hunters in the 1920s and '30s are of particular interest, since this is around the time period my grandfather, Caleb Reding, was in his prime as a hunter, and is a major focus for my writing.

Caleb and Aldo

As I read on, realization grows. For years I have puzzled over my reluctance to write the story of my grandfather's wolf hunting exploits. The stories of his hunting, my too-brief time with him, my mother's adoring recounting of her childhood times with her father; all have been very compelling to me. Russell's essays help clarify that reluctance. All small boys, all children, need heroes; it is part of our search for identity, of basic personality formation. I found one in Caleb Reding. During my childhood, this tall man loomed larger-than-life, as heroes do. The brief time I spent with him, hunting exploits told by family and friends, my mother's adoration—all helped create a hero. He was also a farmer who would often choose a hunt over the plow, sometimes neglecting his family in the bargain. These quirks do not diminish him in my eyes. They serve only to make him more real, to provide a more balanced view.

Who am I to make judgments about this man who was born over a century ago? This cross-timbers section of North Texas was still a frontier when as a young man Papa hunted the rolling prairies, uplands and timbered draws.

From the time he was a young boy he hunted with his father, uncles, cousins, family friends. The tales told around the campfires of Caleb Reding's youth were of Indian raids and cattle drives, as well as of hunts for wolf, cougar and bear. In 1883, the year of his birth, cowmen were pushing the last cattle drives up the Chisholm Trail, which ran a few miles northwest of the Reding family farm near Slidell in Wise County. Ten years earlier, Comanche and Kiowa war parties were still raiding this part of Texas. My grandfather would see the end of the Texas frontier, the fencing of the range, and with it, the end of the wolf in this part of Texas.

If I could reach back through those six decades that now separate us and touch him, speak to him, what would I say? As an environmentalist, I deplore the eradication and near-extinction of so many forms of wildlife, particularly the wolf. But this old wolf hunter was a man of his time, as I am of mine, and that time chasm cannot be spanned. But my bet is we would find many points of agreement, especially if he could know all that has transpired in those intervening 60 years regarding the near-extinction of the wolf in the lower 48. He was a sportsman, like my brother is today; no sportsman wants any game animal to be extinct. I believe he would also be an advocate for reintroducing the wolf into the western wilderness.

There is a parallel life channeled near Caleb's, like two rivers running near each other but never intersecting. In my alternate universe these two lives would intersect: "Papa, say 'hello' to Aldo Leopold."

Caleb Reding and Aldo Leopold were born within a couple of years of each other, lived their formative years in the southwest, hunters whose encounters with wolves, for Leopold at least, caused a personal transformation which pioneered the conservation and ecology movements into the powerful forces of today. A seminal moment early in his U.S. Forest Service career is chronicled in his lyrical, profound epic, *A Sand County Almanac:*

> *A deep chesty bawl echoes from rimrock to rimrock, rolls down the mountain, and fades into the far blackness of the night. It is an outburst of wild defiant sorrow, and of contempt for all the adversities of the world.*
>
> *Every living thing (and perhaps many a dead one as well) pays heed to that call. To the deer it is a reminder of the way of all flesh, to the pine a forecast of midnight scuffles and of*

blood upon the snow, to the coyote a promise of gleanings to come, to the cowman a threat of red ink at the bank, to the hunter a challenge of fang against bullet. Yet behind these obvious and immediate hopes and fears there lies a deeper meaning, known only to the mountain itself. Only the mountain has lived long enough to listen objectively to the howl of a wolf.

Those unable to decipher the hidden meaning know nevertheless that it is there, for it is felt in all wolf country . . . . It tingles in the spine of all who hears wolves by night, or who scan their tracks by day. Even without sight or sound . . . it is implicit in a hundred small events: the midnight whinny of a pack horse, the rattle of rolling rocks, the bound of a fleeing deer, the way shadows lie under the spruces. Only the ineducable can fail to sense the presence or absence of wolves, or the fact that mountains have a secret opinion about them.

My own conviction on this score dates from the day I saw a wolf die. We were eating lunch on a high rimrock, at the foot of which a turbulent river elbowed its way. We saw what we thought was a doe fording the torrent, her breast awash in white water. When she climbed the bank toward us and shook out her tail, we realized our error: it was a wolf. A half-dozen others, evidently grown pups, sprang from the willows and all joined in a welcoming melee of wagging tails and playful maulings. What was literally a pile of wolves writhed and tumbled in the center of an open flat at the foot of our rimrock.

In those days we had never heard of passing up a chance to kill a wolf. In a second we were pumping lead into the pack . . . . When our rifles were empty, the old wolf was down, and a pup was dragging a leg into impassable slide-rocks.

We reached the old wolf in time to watch a fierce green fire dying in her eyes. I realized then, and have known ever since, that there was something new to me in those eyes— something known only to her and to the mountain. I was young then, and full of trigger-itch; I thought that because fewer wolves meant more deer, that no wolves would mean hunters' paradise. But after seeing the green fire die, I sensed that neither the wolf nor the mountain agreed with such a view.

This wolf encounter would later be reported as a major influence on Leopold's shift toward a more naturalistic view of wildlife and wilderness; would place him in the vanguard of believers in preserving the land and native animals, and along with Thoreau he became a major spokesman for Thoreau's dictum:

In wildness is the salvation of the world.

4.

And my campfire tales? They are tame in comparison to my grandfather's, but thrilling enough for me. Just being there was a thrill, forget about the stories told. I don't remember any of them now.

But thanks to my mom's tellings and my journal notes there is much I do remember. Sitting around a crackling fire, the smell of strong coffee from a large, fire-blackened coffee pot, getting my own tin cup, scalding, too hot to hold, too bitter to drink, and wonderful! I remember the laughter and jocular behavior among the men seated around the fire who had done this same thing many times. The camaraderie of the hunt, listening to the distant baying, each owner having the uncanny ability (to me) to recognize each dog's yelp or howl, what the different hound sounds meant. "That's ole Blue. He's picked up the scent." Or, "Trixie's on it now. She'll find that fox for sure." And sometime later, the one they had all been listening for—hounds now baying an octave higher: "They got 'im, he's treed! Let's go, boys, before he gits away!"

Then the dash to put out the fire, collect coffee pot and other possibles, figure out the best way to get from here to there, what roads to take, whose place the treed or cornered fox was likely to be on. It was all done with practiced ease and economy of effort, seeming mystical to my five-year-old mind. By the time I could climb up into the cab of the Model A Ford pickup, we were off. In truth, of the too-few times I got to go hunting with Papa, only once did the hounds catch, or tree, a fox. The other times, we went home empty handed, usually not until very late, after the hounds had hunted for much of the night. On those occasions, knowing there would be no fox caught this night, Papa would get his fox horn from the pickup, and blow a loud, piercing series of notes.

His horn, carved from the horn of a steer by a cousin, was a prized possession, one I secretly coveted. Each time I came for a visit I tried to blow it, but never successfully. I came to believe that the day I could blow the notes Papa blew would mark my entry into manhood. That horn now occupies a place of honor in my home, and after practice over the years I can blow a passable imitation of Caleb's call to the hounds. I hope Papa can hear the notes I blow. I'll bet he can.

Not long after the horn blew, the hounds would come straggling in over a period of time, in pairs or one by one. Some, refusing to give up the hunt, would be left to find their way home, often limping in with thorns in their paws, footsore, tongues lolling, heads down, "dog tired". On most occasions, having sat around the campfire listening to the hunter's stories and to the dogs baying in the distance as long as I could, I would fall asleep, sometimes on my grandfather's knee, sometimes on the ground. Try as is might, I just couldn't seem to stay awake all night like the men did. It became a point of honor to stay awake like the big guys. One night, well after midnight, when Papa's horn-blowing jolted me awake, I jumped up and said, "I didn't go to sleep this time, did I Papa?"

"Naw, son, ya did jist fine," he said, patting my shoulder, a smile creasing his sun-browned face. I was very proud.

My mother tells about going hunting with Papa a few times, a rare privilege for a girl in those days.

Something of a tomboy, and Papa's favorite, she often helped with the outside chores and field work while her older sister, Beula, helped my grandmother with kitchen chores and housework. Mom had similar feelings to mine regarding the hunter's camaraderie and campfire tales. She also recounts her pleasure at taking Papa's saddle horse, Mouse, down to the creek to wash him off after a long, muddy hunt. The hunters would frequently go on a hunt after a rain, wolf sign easier for the hounds to pick up and track, the fields too muddy to work in. It was a task other siblings were not allowed to do; Mom felt special for being allowed to do it.

By the time I came along a generation later, Mouse had been replaced by a Model A pickup, the rolling, open savannahs and wooded streams of North Central Texas were being criss-crossed by fences, the wolf was gone and game of any kind was scarce. In the fall of 1941, when I went on my last hunt with him, Caleb Reding was 58 years old and had hunted regularly for five decades. He had collected bounties on or sold the hides of an untold number of wolves, foxes, badgers and cougars caught in that rugged cross-timbers country.

Caleb became known as one of the best hunters in that area of Texas. My mom recalls that as a girl, she would answer the door knock of a rancher or farmer. "Is this where the wolf hunter lives?" asking for my grandfather to come to their place to track down a wolf who had killed livestock. And later, just a wolf sighting reported by an anxious farmer was enough to bring the dogs out on a hunt. Later still, the wolves now gone, the hunters still hungry for the chase, they switched to tracking less-predatory game such as fox or an occasional badger. By the time I came along, the gray and Mexican red wolf had been all but eradicated from that part of Texas. A few lone stragglers remained. I saw one in November, 1941.

But I am here to recount remembrances as a grandson, so what questions do I ask him now? Thinking about this for a while, I have some. Did you ever get tired of the killing? Did you ever look a captured wolf in the eyes, and just before death, wonder at the intelligence you saw there, that "dying green fire?" Did you know or think about any of the wolf's similarities to us: his fierce loyalty to his family, her gentle indulgence with her pups, how much of a family man he is? If you knew, what did you think about it? These, and more, come to mind.

My brother Jerry, a few years younger, is a successful small-businessman, a life-long hunter and sportsman. He and a couple of friends have long-standing game leases in South Texas and Central Texas, where they spend several weeks each year during the various hunting seasons of deer, quail, dove, javelina. My grandfather would have been proud of him. Of me, perhaps less so, because I'm not a hunter, have not picked up a gun to kill something since I was thirteen years old.

One chilly fall day our family went to visit my aunt and uncle, Roberta and Bob Buchanan, on their dairy farm southwest of Decatur. I was an eighth grader now and had taken along Dad's Marlin 22-caliber lever-action rifle, a beauty I had always admired, probably because it looked a lot like Red Ryder's 30-30 rifle. I wandered off through the pasture and down into the woods, occasionally plinking away at inanimate targets.

Deeper in the woods now, I began looking up into the tall oaks scanning for squirrels or their nests.

Mom had said she would skin and fry up any squirrels I shot. I didn't like squirrel fried or fricasseed, but thought I might bring one or two back if any were seen. Spotting one scampering up a nearby oak I aimed but didn't shoot: too quick to draw a bead on. Further along I saw a nest and aimed a shot into the nest, the lazy boy's way, but nothing there. Further still, high up into a tall oak, leaves mostly fallen, I saw another nest and fired away. The screeching wail from the nest is one I'll never forget, sounding like the cry of a seriously injured child. Staggered by the almost-human scream, I dropped the Marlin into a pile of autumn leaves. Not one but two squirrels plummeted to the ground, their bodies crunching into leaves nearby. One fluffy tail twitched a long time, then stilled.

No more squirrel hunting for me. It was a long walk back to the warm kitchen.

There is a division around hunting among my children as well. My oldest son, Mark, likes to hunt and has gone with my brother on several occasions. My other three children are or have been vegetarians.

As seen through my five-year-old eyes, this land still seemed wild and exotic. But by 1941, hunters on horseback were stymied by barbed wire, having to go farther afield to find good hunting grounds, and having to travel on country roads instead of following the hounds on horseback across open fields and woodland as they had done in earlier days when the game was more plentiful, the countryside still open and unfenced as much of it had come to be in those pre-World War II years.

The frontier of my grandfather's youth was ending by the time he came of age, at seventeen marrying my grandmother, Virginia Myers, age fifteen, in the spring of 1901. By the time I came along two generations later, the frontier was gone, and I had heard familiar lamentations around a hunters' campfire: hardly any game anymore; most of the land fenced-in now; unable to ride free across hill-and-dale, pounding in pursuit of a pack of hounds hot on the trail of a wolf. More than once I heard a hunter curse "that damn 'bob-wire'". Caleb Reding longed for those earlier days of abundant game and unfettered prairies. So do I, but for different reasons.

5.

<u>2002, Redux</u>

It is now Monday, the weather has cleared and I head west into a brisk, chill wind to Decatur for visits with my two aunts, the only remaining relatives who may be able to fill in some of the spaces of Gage family history I do not have. I am trying to gather some more specifics, to fill in memory gaps regarding my grandparents, particularly my Grandfather Merlin.

My parents have given me very little to go on. My father, a man of few words, never had a bad thing to say about anyone, and rarely spoke of his father. Over the years my mother, also taciturn and not one to gossip, has had little to say about him, but yesterday as we reminisced about those early times, she opened up in a way I had never heard before.

She told of how in 1934, not long after their marriage, they went to the Gage family farm to pick up a hog to sell, one given to Dad as a piglet which he had raised, cared for and fed for a couple of years—a prize boar he had shown at the Denton County Fair. Upon arriving at the farm, they found that my grandfather had sold the boar the day before and pocketed the $12 he got from the sale.

I hear the resentment in Mom's voice as she finishes this revelation: "It was a selfish, mean thing to do, Jimmy. We had just married, were dead broke, JG had worked like a dog for that man his whole life, and that's the thanks he got." After this new and surprising information, Mom pauses here, as if maybe she's said too much, then goes on, vitriol still in her voice: "Merlin Gage was supposed to be such a fine Christian man, an Elder in the Church an' all. Well, I never had much respect for him after that, and I think he knew it."

Another pause here, the look of resentment fades into one of sadness, a tear runs down her cheek, she looks away. We are sitting knee to knee; she grips my hand tightly, still looking away, silently imploring me to understand this bitter rancorous kernel she has just coughed up.

I do understand. Twelve dollars was a lot of money in those days, the equivalent of several hundred dollars today. This was the depths of the

Great Depression, and many men were working for a dollar a day or less, if they could find work. In 1940, the year my brother was born, Dad was working on a Wise County road crew 50 hours a week, driving a road grader and other equipment. His pay, funded by the WPA, was thirty dollars a month.

After a long moment of silence, my mother speaks again, voice softer now, perhaps needing to balance her out-of-character harshness toward her father-in-law: "Now your Maw Maw, your Grandmother Buena, was something else; she was as fine a woman as I ever knew, and she thought you and Jerry were about *it*."

I ponder this little unexpected jolt during the short trip to Decatur, set it aside, and settle in with visits with my aunts about their early recollections, hoping to get a more complete picture of my Grandfather Gage than my memory can conjure up, since I was only eight when he died, probably of cancer, in 1944. My scant memories of him are of a sick, frail man, but in old photographs he stands tall, staring back at the camera through dark, deep-set eyes. My aunts recall their father very differently—a hard-working successful farmer and church leader—a beloved father struck down in his prime by a disease little understood 60 years ago. There was no such thing as chemotherapy or related drugs in those days, and from 1939 to 1944 he had a series of five operations. The disease slowly rendered him unable to work, and the Gage family farm was sold in 1943, my grandparents moving to Decatur, where he died at home in December 1944 at the age of 53.

Less than six months later, my favorite grandfather, Caleb Reding, was also dead from cancer.

After my visits with my aunts, Lavada and Roberta, I am reminded anew that two people rarely see things the same way, and these two rarely agree on anything. They don't even agree on the cause of my Grandfather Merlin's death. What I know for sure is that the fathers of both my parents died within a five-month time period, and we moved back to Texas in May, 1945. It was events surrounding the death of my Grandfather Caleb, little understood at the time, which swept us from that arid, smelly El Paso Natural Gas Company camp in Eastern New Mexico back to the rural life I loved, to a small ranch nestled on the rolling prairie west of Ft. Worth.

When I arrive at the Griggs' house they are, as usual, glad to see me. Of all my relatives on both sides of the family, Bill and Lavada Griggs are closest to me. For the first twelve years of their married life they were childless, and treated Jerry and me as if we were their own kids, taking us for extended periods during the summer, and staying in regular contact with us. Lavada, an elementary teacher for over 40 years, was responsible for helping me get my first teaching job in Irving, where she taught for a number of years. During my first year of teaching in 1957, their only child, Melinda, was born. Now retired and living in Decatur where they were both born, with their daughter the High School Principal and two grandsons to spoil and cluck over, they are living out the life of their dreams.

We spend a few minutes getting caught up on family happenings, then decide to take off for the Sycamore Cemetery, where my Gage grandparents are buried, then on to the old Gage home place, now owned by a distant cousin, and to try to find the places where we lived from 1938–42. During our trek around this part of northeast Wise County, Lavada fills me in on a few details I do not have.

Later, I journey five miles southwest of Decatur to the dairy farm of my Aunt Roberta, the other holder of early details about our life in Wise County before World War II. Roberta and Bob Buchanan were married in 1944, just before Bob shipped out to San Diego as a navy seaman. The Buchanans have lived on the same dairy farm for over 50 years, expanding it over time to one of the most successful in North Texas, if not the entire state. At that time they milked 500 jersey cows, employing a large crew of mostly Mexican nationals, some of whom have been working and living on the farm with their families for 30 years. My Aunt Roberta has been the farm's financial and business manager from the beginning, and is one of the finest Christian women I know.

Roberta supplies a few more useful details about my grandfather, some conflicting with those provided by Lavada, and we conclude our visit. I head back on Highway 51 to Slidell, twelve miles northeast of Decatur, making a brief stop at the

cemetery where my Reding grandparents are buried
to check for confirmation of gravestone dates.

6.

The week earmarked for this journey into the past is almost over, so early Friday morning I stop for a visit with Mom before taking off for the trip home to New Mexico. Each return trip to Denton I see her becoming more frail and in poorer health, and not for the first time wonder if this goodbye may be the last. Perhaps because she has revealed some unusually intimate details during the past few days, the leaving today is particularly hard. She has always received good care here at Good Samaritan and the staff loves her, but today the sounds and smells of the aged and infirm, of urine and despair, are almost more than I can bear—nobody gets out of this place alive.

The guilt I feel for keeping my mother in this warehouse of old people waiting to die drives me out the door of her room, then down corridors where I dodge through a human obstacle course of wheelchair-bound captives, and finally out the front door. Tears streaming down my face, gasping for a breath of fresh air, I utter a silent prayer, one so familiar now it has almost become a mantra: *Please, God, don't let me end up like this; old, feeble and unable to take care of myself.* How many of us who have seen our parents grow old and infirm offer a similar prayer, just as fervently held? *Please let me die quickly, and not be a burden to anyone.* Each time my brother and I talk, our conversation invariably comes around to this topic; he feels the same way I do about the end of our lives. After I tell him I have recently renewed my membership in the Hemlock Society, his rejoinder is: "Gittin' old ain't for sissies."

Today the route home takes a different direction, due west toward El Paso. I am taking this detour to a spot in the West Texas desert where I hope to find the El Paso Natural Gas Company camp where we lived in 1942–43. Passing through Decatur, I take Texas 51 toward Weatherford, where it intersects with I-20. After about fifteen minutes, lost in thought and paying little attention to the road ahead, I come very close to disaster.

Traveling along at a good clip, enjoying the countryside, I fail to see the stop sign for an intersecting highway up ahead and blast right through the intersection, realizing too late that I should have stopped, and have to do some quick maneuvering to avoid being broad-sided by an on-coming truck. Lucky to make it through unscathed, I am instantaneously jolted by a blast from the horn of another truck coming from the opposite direction, one I did not see at all, one that came very close to hitting me. Badly shaken, a belated adrenaline rush causing my heart to pound and my hands to shake, I coast to a stop, pull over onto the shoulder of the highway, sit with eyes closed and pulse pounding, hands shaking, waiting for my vital signs to get back to normal. Wow! That was as close a call as I can remember having.

Finally able to resume my journey a few minutes later, I drive more sedately toward the interstate, my focus totally on my driving. A flashback of the near miss scrolls across my field of vision, sending a shudder through my body and momentarily blurring my vision. I have to pull over and stop again. I have two more flashbacks ending in vision-blurring shudders before reaching the I-20 intersection in Weatherford. I've had near misses before, but can't remember being shaken as badly as I am by this one.

A couple of hours later, on I-20 near Abilene, finally able to push this brush with disaster into a corner of my mind, I begin to put the new bits and pieces gleaned this week into some kind of order. Something I had always wondered about, but never asked, was the *why* of our moving to West Texas when my father went to work for EPNG. Did he take the job so he wouldn't have to go into the army? Was it happenstance, or what?

Mom cleared it up: Dad needed a job, and my uncle, Lundy Chambers, now working for EPNG, helped Dad get the job. It was that simple. After he had been working in El Paso for a few months, my father, at age 31, got his army induction notice, and showed it to his boss, who said he didn't have to go. The gas company was an "essential industry" to the war effort; he could be exempted from going, and was.

All the wartime activity swirling around us, from my childhood point of view, had little noticeable impact on our lives. We had been poor before the war, we were poor during the war, and we were poor after the war. But we didn't know we were "poor"—

that was a term only used later by social historians to label us and many others like us, it was not in our lexicon. And by now, we had already moved several times during my young life; another move did not seem so bad.

Other than the train trips we took that were crowded with soldiers as we traveled between El Paso and Ft. Worth, the war went by relatively unnoticed by me. It was only later, as I became older and paid attention to such things, that WW II had an impact. It was the post-war boom of the late '40s and throughout the '50s that I tuned in to.

Being "poor" wasn't something I noticed—everybody we knew was pretty much in the same shape. Yeah, we moved around, my dad going from job to job, but since there was no other point of comparison, I took our lifestyle for granted. Truth is, I didn't think about it—hey, I was just a kid! Maybe we didn't have much money, but we always had food on the table and a roof over our heads, and my mom, an excellent seamstress (and, as I came to realize later, a fashion maven), made sure we were always decked out nicely. I never felt deprived, or less of a person than anyone else. There were lots of families who were less fortunate than we were.

I would not trade my childhood years for anything. Living in the country, roaming free and unfettered, always feeling safe, having loving parents and family, and lots of animals around—what a great way to grow up! Blessed to have had the childhood I had, I wish my children and grandchildren the same safe, secure, loving environment in which to grow. My greatest fears today revolve around the dangerous world our grandchildren will inherit.

On a hot, sultry evening in early August 1936, a couple arrived late for the beginning of services of Summer Revival at the Sycamore Church of Christ. They had visited too long at the home of the Allen's in Justin, and hurried in with news to report. Tonight, the revival meeting had been moved outside to meet under a large brush arbor some church members had completed a few hours earlier. During previous nights of the revival, the heat had been as intense as the fire-and-brimstone sermons, and three women had fainted. Two elders' wives put their heads together, and declared they would be staying home for the final week of the revival unless something was done to cool the small country church house. A hurriedly constructed brush arbor under tall oak trees was the answer.

The first song was ending as the couple found a seat at the back. As the congregation sat down, cardboard fans—a picture of a kneeling Jesus on one side and "Christian Funeral Home, Decatur, Texas" on the other—were much in evidence, vigorous fanning stirring the still, hot air. The woman, a distant family cousin, leaned over to the woman next to her and whispered, "Nona had her baby. It's a boy!"

The evening before, around midnight, JG walked a mile to the home of family friends, the Matthews', to use their telephone to call his cousin, Dr. Joe Allen, who lived in Justin, ten miles away. Dr. Joe was away making a house call, but arrived at sunup. I was born three hours later on the morning of August 3, 1936, in a one-bedroom, dirt-floored cabin on the WR Ranch, where my father worked as a ranch hand. The ranch was near Argyle, a small community halfway between Ft. Worth and Denton. When I was born, my parents had been married three years and had moved four times. By the time we moved to Denton in 1948, we had moved another seven times. My vagabond life began early.

I remember none of those early moves, but I do recall Christmas 1940 for two reasons: a new arrival in the family—my baby brother Jerry was born ten days before Christmas, red-faced but still very cute; and I got a new single-shot BB gun. I had wanted what every boy at the time wanted—a Red

Ryder BB gun, but I loved my new single shot, so much that I had to try it out immediately. We were going to the Gage family Christmas, and I was eager to show off my new weapon. I went to wait in the car, could not resist trying it out, so put it up to the backseat car window and fired, just to see what it would do. Well, you probably know what happened! I didn't get to take my prized new present to the family gathering; was probably lucky my dad was in a holiday spirit so didn't get my butt busted. Having to leave it at home was punishment enough.

8.

Buster and Maw Maw

For the first few years of my life my best friend and constant companion was my dog, Buster. Mom and Dad got him as a pup before I was old enough to walk; he the unwanted offspring from a litter of my grandfather Caleb's hunting dogs. Seems one of his fox terrier females got out of her pen and fell in love for the night with a handsome foreign devil, a German Shepherd, and Buster was the love child of this coupling. He may not have been wanted by my grandfather, but he was wanted, and loved, by me.

We developed a bond so strong my mother often checked on my whereabouts while I was outside playing, invisible in the tall prairie grass, by locating Buster, whose regular leaps above the grass, searching for prey, made his presence known. Mom knew I would be nearby; Buster went everywhere with me.

Buster was a handsome devil himself, a tan and gray version of the "ole yeller dog" of Walt Disney fame. He had the intelligence and indomitable spirit of Ole Yeller as well. A born hunter, he often returned from daily forays into the countryside with the canine version of a satisfied grin. I thought him a great hunter, a great dog.

When I was four years old, my dad bought me a red wagon, a Radio Flyer, and made a leather harness for Buster, who wasn't thrilled with his new role as wagon dog. With some practice around the yard, closely supervised by my parents, he finally gave in and pulled me lots of places.

On a lovely spring day a few weeks later, I hitched Buster to my wagon and took off to visit to my Gage grandparents, whose farm was about a mile down the road. Packed for an overnight stay, we headed out down the road, Buster dutifully pulling me, always on the lookout. Things were going great until we got about halfway there, when a jackrabbit ran across the road. His first calling had always been hunter, not wagon-puller, so off he took after the rabbit, forgetting he was firmly attached to a wagon with me in it. Well, not so firmly, as it turned out. The rabbit chaser bolted across the road, leaped the bar ditch, made it—and so did the wagon, but not the rider. I ended up at the bottom of the ditch, scratched, upset, but unhurt.

Retrieving the wagon, torn from Buster's harness by the fence across the ditch, and gathering my overnight belongings, I snuffled and shuffled on down the road to Maw Maw Gage's house. My grief and consternation at the wagon wreck were somewhat mollified by the milk and cookies she always had available for me. I didn't try the wagon trek with Buster again.

It is now summer, August, and I am standing at the back door of Maw Maw's kitchen. She has emptied enough fresh milk from the morning's milking to fill the crock churn. I lean over to smell the creamy milk; it smells warm, alive, sweet like clover.

This tiny, beloved woman, always moving, always busy, asks me if I would like to churn the butter. I'm very excited, but can only smile and nod timidly. She fits the wooden paddle through the hole in the top of the churn, puts her hand over mine, shows me how to move the ladle slowly up and down, up and down, up and down. I do this on my own for what seems an eternity. My arm, then both arms, are now tired.

"How you doin', Son? Need some help?" I don't say anything, keep moving the ladle up and down, labored now. She gently takes the handle, finishes churning the butter, pours off the clabbered milk, then gives me a finger-full of fresh butter. The taste is rich, creamy, delicious. And I did it (almost) by myself!

Backward, turn backward, O Time in your flight,
Make me a child again just for tonight.

Anonymous

Many years later I stand in this same spot, same house, now a falling-down shell, looking back through the years with a clarity like yesterday, seeing the kitchen, the backdoor, behind it the summer kitchen where she did all her summer and fall harvest canning. Going to the cistern, pulling up the spring box from the cool depths, she puts the freshly churned butter in the tray. Lowering it back down she looks north, down toward the fields ringed by the creek, where the harvest crew is threshing oats in the stifling late summer Texas heat.

I don't remember the steamy heat of that day—all these years later my memory is only of the good things: The smells, feels, secretive tastes of fresh butter and peaches, the earthy sweet smell of freshly picked ears of corn; a high, thin, tangy smell I now know to be vinegar mixed with sugar and spices for the pickled peaches on the day's canning and preserving agenda. It was a special day with Maw Maw and me alone together doing a woman's summer harvest work.

9.

*We humans fear the beast within the wolf
because we do not understand the beast within
ourselves*

Gerald Hausman, *Turtle Island Alphabet*

A gray, blustery day before Thanksgiving, 1941. I am up, early and eager. The night before, Dad had said he would take me with him to gather pecans for Mom's holiday cooking needs. He knew of a small grove of native pecan trees in a pasture not far from our house. I was feeling very grown up and excited by the prospect of walking with my father across the rolling countryside to collect this fall bounty. It is the first time I recall just the two of us going out like this. Of course, Buster would go with us.

Time has dimmed all but a few of those long-ago memories, but two events from that day remain as vivid today as they were then: The first is of collecting pecans. We walked for what seemed a long time before we came to the pecan grove. I smelled it before I saw it—a chill, moist wind carried the tannic, distinctive pecans-in-their-hulls aroma beckoned from just over a rise. There were no more than half a dozen native pecans trees, not large, but loaded with pecans still in their hulls. Dad found a long, dead branch and began *frailing* them from the higher limbs while I stretched up to shake some of the lower limbs to get the pecans to fall onto the ground. As they fell into the tall grass under the trees, I got down on my hands and knees to collect the fallen nuts. We had brought a couple of paper sacks which we soon filled with the small, thick-shelled nuts. Dad showed me how to crack a pecan, but I was not very good at it, so he shelled a few for me to eat. The pecan taste was strong and delicious.

Buster was off on one of his usual forays, looking for a rabbit, a skunk, anything he could chase. For some dog reason I could never understand, he loved to kill skunks, and even though he frequently got sprayed, which resulted in him foaming at the mouth like a rabid dog, he never quit skunk hunting. Just as we finished filling up the last sack, he trotted back to the pecan grove, jumped a jackrabbit and tore off after it, straining and whining in hot pursuit, disappearing over a hill to the north. Sometimes he was successful at jackrabbit hunting as well.

As we began our journey back home, Dad spotted a persimmon tree in the distance, east of our route toward the house. We detoured to the persimmon tree and found it loaded with ripe fruit. Since our paper bags were filled with pecans, we had nowhere to put anything else, so we crammed our pockets with pecans from the paper sacks to make room for the unexpected bounty. Putting squishy persimmons in your pants pocket is not a good idea. Perhaps I had eaten a persimmon before, but this was the first time I *remember* eating one. After putting as many on top of the pecans as we could, Dad took off the felt hat he always wore and we began filling it with the ripe fruit, and eating some too. I picked a large, firm one and bit into it: Wow, what a pucker! If you've ever bitten into a not-quite-ripe persimmon, you know what I mean.

We filled Dad's hat with the fruit, picking mostly ripe ones that had fallen, half-hidden, into the tall grass under the tree, then headed toward home. The sky, which had begun the day with high clouds scudding in from the north, was lower now and darker, the chill wind blowing harder. I was now shivering from the cold, a damp wind gusting from the north, so we began moving quickly toward home, ready for the warmth of Mom's kitchen.

Trailing single-file through the tall, autumn grasses, me in the lead now, Dad holding back, we came to a gentle rise that fell off into a wrinkle in the landscape, a tiny stream creasing through it. I was walking several yards ahead of my father, looking around for Buster, who had streaked off after the jackrabbit and had not been seen since. I wasn't worried. He always came back after his frequent hunting trips.

Suddenly, silently, he was there beside me, behaving strangely. He seemed to slink up, his body lower to the ground. He stopped right in front of me, body rigid, tail down, the hair on his back standing up, staring at something across the meandering creeklet. Something was up. I stopped by his side and looked where my pal was looking. For a few moments I saw nothing but the fall landscape, all tans, browns and grays, blending at the horizon into a threatening pewter sky.

I noticed the amber eyes first, riveted on me, or maybe Buster, piercing the chill, damp air across the swale that separated us, perhaps 40 yards away. I saw his head next, turned toward me, partially hidden by the tall grasses. Then I noticed his lean body and long, gangly legs. My brain finally registered that the animal had been there all the time, camouflaged by the color of his pelt, blending perfectly with his surroundings.

He looked huge, bigger than Buster, my only point of reference. Buster was a big dog, weighing 60-70 pounds. I stood there, spellbound in that magical moment, unable to move, starring across the creek as the gray wolf's luminous eyes flared back at me. Maybe it wasn't me he glared at, but Buster. For at my side, leaning into me, Buster was also motionless and silent, his canine wisdom telling him that he was no match for this wild brother who could probably tear him to pieces. It was the only time in our many adventures together I had known him not to take off after another canine.

I can't tell you how long that brief encounter lasted. Einstein was right; time is relative. What now seems like a long time was probably only a few seconds, maybe less, and then the spell was broken as my Dad walked up behind us. He stopped as I raised my arm and pointed.

"Look, Daddy, I think it's a wolf!" I whispered. He said nothing, tried to focus on the spot where I pointed. In that brief moment the gray shape shifted, vanishing back into the tall grass. Buster moved beside me and broke his silence with a low whine, the hair on his back still high-ridged. He made no effort to give chase.

Rooted in that spot, I continued to stare across the creek, eyes searching for another glimpse, but he was gone.

"I don't see anything, son. Come on, let's git home, it's about to rain," my father coaxed, placing a hand on my shoulder, then walking away. Reluctantly, I turned to follow, Buster now trotting closely on my father's heels.

On the trek back I tried to talk about what we had seen. But my father's quiet nature and the necessity of walking single file through the tall, thick grasses of the pasture combined to elicit only a few non-committal sounds: "Uh, huh;" "I don't know, Jimmy," and "Maybe it was another dog." This last phrase stopped me. I *knew* it wasn't another dog, and so did Buster. If it had been another dog, Buster would have been after it in a flash. On more than one occasion I had seen him hurl himself into dogfights without regard to the odds, once flying into a pack of hounds, emerging from the melee with his satisfied dog smile and no notable harm.

Almost home, damp and chilled from the misty rain that had begun to fall, I ran ahead to tell my mother about what we had seen. "Momma, we saw a wolf! He was big!" This as I scurried through the back door into the warm kitchen, putting my pecan/persimmon bag on the table and emptying my pockets. Familiar supper smells mingled with a smoky overlay from the wood cook-stove my mother labored over. I was hungry after our adventurous outing. Something delicious baked in the oven, but my eyes were drawn to the skillet that held her undivided attention on the stovetop—she was making apricot fried pies, a speciality of hers, a favorite of mine.

As I held out my hands to warm them near the stove chimney, I noticed my baby brother, Jerry, under the kitchen table happily banging away on kitchen pans, a large spoon in each hand. Almost a year old, he now moved around enough to need constant attention, a job I sometimes was asked to do.

As my father entered the kitchen, I said, "Tell her, Daddy, tell Mama about the wolf we saw." He put the nut and fruit bounty we had collected on the kitchen table and stood behind me, holding his hands above mine next to the hot chimney. "Jimmy thinks he saw a wolf on our way home. I'm not sure. Whatever it was moved away before I got a good look."

"I did see one. Buster saw it, too." Stung by my father's doubting tone, I tried to move away from him, leaning into my mother's flour-covered apron.

"Look out, son, this grease is hot, it'll burn you," my mother said, paying not nearly enough attention to my important announcement and not taking her eyes off the sizzling skillet, deftly flipping the golden half-moon pies. I moved back from the stove, sullen now that neither parent seemed to be on my side in the wolf matter.

"Let me finish with these pies." A quick glance in my direction pried out of her: "I think Papa and his huntin' buddies cleaned out the wolves in this country when I was still a girl." As I was about to protest, she looked over her shoulder at me again, noting my down-in-the-mouth look and added, gently this time: "I guess there still could be an old lone wolf or two around." This was sounding better.

"Papa" was her father, Caleb Redding, my grandfather and hero, someone who loomed larger-than-life in my world. I spent as much time with him as I could, loving every minute of our time together, no matter how menial or hard the task: riding beside or behind him as he plowed his fields with Doc and John, a matched pair of bay work horses, sometimes allowed to ride to town in the back of his old Model A pickup, dodging the spurts of tobacco juice that he spat out at regular intervals.

But the thing I loved more than anything else was to go fox hunting with Papa and his hunting buddies. Having only recently achieved this exalted status, at age five, of going on an all-night fox hunt with this band of hunters, my grandfather the undisputed leader, I thought I knew a thing or two about the critters men hunted, and wolves in particular. Why wolves? Well, therein lies the tale.

10.

<u>Caleb's Horn</u>

In his prime, Caleb Redding was something of a regional hunting legend in this part of North Texas, encompassing several counties south of the Red River, the natural boundary between Texas and Oklahoma. By the time he turned seventeen and married my grandmother in 1901, he had helped hunt, track, trap, and collect the bounty on dozens of wolves. Over the next twenty-odd years he would catch dozens more. By the time I was born, the wolf population of North Texas had been almost extinguished, and he had switched to hunting other game: fox, coyote, badger, an occasional cougar.

For most of his earlier life, Caleb had hunted wolves on horseback with a pack of wolf hounds, the land still mostly open and not yet circumscribed by fences. He still used a pack of hounds for fox hunting, but now, two generations later, he took his fox hounds to the hunting site in a specially built cage which slid into the bed of his Model A pickup. Arriving at a likely spot, the tightly packed hounds were released, and in joyous confusion at being set free to do what they were bred for, put their noses to the ground, sniffing in all directions for scent of game. After quartering the area, this howling scramble, now enlarged by the other hunters' dogs, would soon find a scent and off they loped behind the leader, noses down, whippet tails lashing the night air, woofing and baying in an off-key, canine chorus. Papa and his hunting cronies would stand around for a while, listening for the purposeful howls that said the dogs were tracking a scent. If satisfied, the guys would then rustle up dead branches, build a campfire, and make a big pot of camp coffee. While sitting around the fire, listening for the baying of the hounds, they told stories about memorable hunts and the dogs who hunted with them. My grandfather was a great storyteller.

Looking back at that long-ago time, everything seemed larger than life to that five-year-old boy. I was an honored guest in the presence of giants.

I say that Papa and his buddies were hunters, but the dogs were the real hunters. They did all the tracking and chasing up to the moment when an animal was treed, or cornered in a den, or as sometimes happened, evaded the hounds and got away. In Caleb Redding's world, hunting dogs were prized possessions, carefully bred, trained and well-cared for.

My grandfather's regional fame as a hunter had as much to do with the excellent hunting dogs he raised and trained as with his prowess as a tracker and hunter. In those days, hunters were known for the hounds they raised and hunted with, not so much for their sharpshooting skills.

Papa's devotion to hunting shaped a good portion of his life. He was a farmer only when he had to be, which was most of the time, but his love of hunting, hunting dogs and the society of men who shared his passion for the sport would often win out over domestic duties. This passion for hunting and the hounds he raised was a source of conflict between him and my grandmother.

Early one morning, after he had just come home from an all night hunt, he insisted on making large pans of cornbread to feed the dogs—no Dog Chow or Kibbles back then—before Mama could fix breakfast for the family. I overheard her say: "Caleb, you take care of those dogs better than you do your own family."

"Aw, hell, Jennie," he replied, "they're family, too."

My favorite part of the few hunting trips I was allowed to go on with Papa was sitting around the campfire as the men talked and told stories, listening to the hounds baying in the distance. Each hunter knew his dog's bark or howl and what those sounds meant. "There's ole Blue," or "Doc's in the lead now," or "Rambler's found a new scent." How could they know what was going on just from listening to the hounds' baying and barking? It all seemed like magic to my young ears.

When the dogs had treed or grounded a fox the baying became more intense, taking on an urgent shrillness that even I could recognize. Then the men sprang to action, taking off in the direction of the cornered animal. On one occasion, we took off across rugged country, driving as close as we could, then bushwhacking to the hounds. They had treed a fox. He was high up in a tall oak tree, terrified. One of the younger, more agile men climbed up the tree, tow sack in his hand, to try to catch the frightened little critter. When he had climbed about half way up, the fox leaped out of the oak, landed on the lower branches of an adjoining tree, then fell to the ground. Quick as a wink the hounds were on him, but just as quick Papa waded into the snarling pack, peeling dogs off the doomed creature. He managed to stuff the half-dead fox into a burlap feed sack and held it high over his head out of the reach of the yelping hounds.

"Too damn scarce to kill," was his comment. By the time I was old enough to be taken on hunting trips, the countryside for many miles around had been mostly "hunted out"; uninjured animals that were caught or trapped were released to be hunted again. The fox was taken home by a cousin to be nursed back to health. If he survived, he would be released, perhaps to be caught again. This was the only time I hunted with Papa that a fox was caught. When I saw the torn and bloody body of the tiny animal before it was placed in the tow sack I hid my eyes, hoping it would survive.

On other hunts no game was scented or caught, so the hounds had to be called in on Papa's hunting horn, carved from a steer antler by one of Mama's nephews. His unforgettable, high, fluting wail to bring the dogs in was one I could never duplicate, try as I might. It took an adult's tight-lipped blow, one I could only muster years later, long after his appreciative ears were available to hear it.

This horn was a plain vanilla replacement for an earlier, fancy one. Mom told this tale:

When Caleb was a young man he had already begun to acquire some regional notoriety, not only as a hunter and tracker but also as an excellent trainer of wolf and fox hounds. As a boy he had been schooled by a series of skilled and demanding family members—father, grandfather, uncles. These men were from a long line of hunters traced back through the family migratory route originating in the Carolinas and Tennessee, back before the Civil War to the early 1800s.

Both sides of our family are of English origin. Caleb was one of the last Redings to remain in rural Texas his whole life. Most of the children and grandchildren would eventually end up in towns and cities—only Lela (Sis) and Hubert, the two oldest children, remained as farmers or ranchers.

The hunting dogs he trained were sometimes sold to other hunters for premium prices; he always kept the best hounds for himself, or sometimes for a cousin or nephew. The pick of the litter he kept for himself.

But how to determine who the best hunters were? Well, by those who trained and hunted with them, or the ultimate measure: By winning a hunting contest, which Papa had done several times.

The fancy horn had been awarded, along with a $25 prize for his dogs, or in this case dog, a beautiful black and tan hound named Trixie. Caleb hunted with her, and a number of her pups and their pups, for many years. As this story unfolds I remember Papa's favorite, Trixie, by then probably a third generation hound in the pack he hunted with when I had gone with him.

This new horn was the real prize, according to Mom, who had admired it as it occupied a place of honor on the mantle in the living room. This beautiful horn was totally filigreed with scrimshaw and silver inlay. Mom, like me two decades later, tried unsuccessfully to blow the horn as a kid.

Papa had said: "It don't blow as good as my old 'un, but it shore is purty!"

But showy, beautiful things have a way of disappearing. The President of the Krum Bank was a sometimes hunting buddy and had a couple of Caleb's dogs. He brought the horn to town for a Show-and-Tell and was asked to let the banker display the horn in his office in a place of honor. How could he refuse? Papa left the horn at the bank, and was told a few weeks later by the bank president that someone had stolen the horn out of his office.

The hunting trips I went on with my grandfather were too few and ended too soon. A few weeks after I saw the wolf, Pearl Harbor was bombed. The family dislocations the war brought would end those special times together with my grandfather, and take us away from the wooded hills and rolling prairie of Wise and Denton counties. When I returned to this part of Texas at the end of the war, he was gone. Memories of those rare, precious times together will be with me always.

11.

The War Years

Twentieth Century social historians have said that without World War II, the Great Depression might have continued for another ten years. The truth of this will never be known, but there were untold thousands of families like ours in Texas and throughout the Southwest who were living on the thin edge of poverty in 1941. The Japanese bombing of Pearl Harbor and Hitler's War changed all that.

In June, 1942, my father left the farm for the first time in his life to work for El Paso Natural Gas Company. An uncle, Lundy Chambers, the husband of my mother's younger sister, Gladys, had gone to work for EPNG the year before, helped get Dad this job. His starting pay was $60 a month.

In August, Mom, Jerry and I moved 500 miles west to join my father. I was now six years old and ready to begin first grade. My brother Jerry was a toddler. Nothing about the war had connected with my world until now. With the move west, things began to change. Looking back down that corridor of time, there is no sense of displacement or trauma, but I did miss my grandparents, and of course, Buster.

Playmates were rare in my rural world—Jerry, four-and-a-half years younger, wouldn't qualify as one for several years. As a solitary child, the adventures Buster and I shared were mythic in my world. That we were leaving him in the care of my grandfather Caleb helped ease, somewhat, the loss of my best friend.

My Grandmother Gage, though small in stature, loomed large as someone else I would sorely miss. As Maw Maw's first, and for almost five years only grandchild, she included me in many memorable firsts: churning butter, making cookies, baking, canning, and one other first, a scary one.

One sultry August afternoon, I must have just turned four or five, she had put me down for a nap I didn't want to take—it was too hot—when she came to tell me to get up and come with her. She took me by the hand and quickly led me through the house, out the back door to the summer kitchen where she was making pickled peaches, a favorite treat. She handed me a piece of cornbread and a couple of fresh peaches, then said, "Wait here, I'll be right back." Inside the house, I heard windows being closed and the front door slammed shut.

A minute later she returned with an oil lamp. "There's a bad storm coming, we have to go to the cellar."

She pointed to the northwest, beyond the arbor covered with cut tree branches that shaded an outdoor cook-stove and large table used for cooking and eating meals during hot summer months. The sky was black, with purple and green hues I had never seen before. Maw Maw looked scared, so I was, too. She hurried me past the cistern to the door of the cellar, sunk into the ground at a 45 degree angle, as huge raindrops began to pop noisily on the metal covering. Grunting with effort, she swung the heavy door open, motioning me to enter. Taking a step downward into the cool, musty opening, something sharp hit me on the back of the neck—ouch, it hurt! Immediately, marble-sized hailstones, and some the size of golf balls, began thundering down, bouncing off the ground, ripping through the arbor brush covering of the summer kitchen. I saw nothing else as I was shoved down into the dank, cool depths, my grandmother closing the door behind her with a thud, hailstones now pinging off the metal cellar door.

I could see nothing; it was pitch black down here. Shivering from the cool, damp air, I was really scared now. Maw Maw pulled me close, held me tight. Her apron smelled of peaches, cinnamon, and cloves. Surrounded by her warmth, I felt better. After a few moments my eyes adjusted to the dark, and I could just make out row upon row of Mason jars filled with canned vegetables and fruit lining the cellar walls on three sides. A long, narrow bench ran along one wall, and at the back, a cot filled the space. My grandmother moved to the side bench, struck a kitchen match, another, then another before finally getting one to light in the damp air. She lit the oil lamp, replaced the chimney, adjusted the wick, and dark corners were filled with lamplight. Perhaps I had been down here before, but never for this long, with this much light. This was also a place of shelter, and I now felt safe, even with the storm thundering outside. A few minutes later, I fell asleep on the cot, my head in my grandmother's lap.

When I awoke sometime later, the storm had passed, bright sunlight was shining down into the cellar. Moving up the cellar steps I saw a broom that lay drying in the sun; Maw Maw had used it a few minutes before to sweep rainwater and storm debris off the floor of the summer kitchen. I grabbed it, now my trusty steed, jumped on and galloped across the yard—riding on Merlin's broom!

12.

The trek west seemed like an adventure. Mom drove our Chevy pulling a trailer loaded with our possessions, stopping only for gas and potty breaks through the heat of the day and a cooler evening. We moved into a wartime tract house in Sunrise Acres, on the eastern edge of El Paso. It was the first time we had ever lived in a town. At that time El Paso was a raw, booming, wartime border town of 75,000, recently swelling with the influx of soldiers and their families who came to the large military training base at Ft. Bliss. Countless thousands of soldiers and airmen were trained there in the vast desert expanse during the war years, and for many years afterward.

A few prominent memories remain from that year in El Paso. One weekend soon after arriving, we made our first trip to Mexico, walking across the bride over the Rio Grande River to Juarez. On the Mexican side of the bridge, Mexican boys dove from a large rock into the clear waters of the river, retrieving pennies tourists threw into the river. The boys, wet brown bodies shiny and slick as seals, would dive down, pick up a coin from the sandy bottom, then come grinning to the surface, holding the shiny coin aloft.

Since that long ago day I have crossed the Rio Grande many times to Juarez and other Mexican destinations. With each crossing I always look to see if the river is clear enough to dive for pennies. It never is. The Rio Grande is now one of the most polluted and threatened rivers in North America.

My first day of school arrived with a bang. I don't remember much about my first teacher or classroom, except that she was large, wore a rusty black dress, and there were too many kids. There must have been forty of us crammed into a classroom built for about half that number. I was one of the lucky ones—I had a desk. Kids who came later in the day were seated on the floor at back, or beneath the chalkboards along one side of the room.

At lunchtime, we took our sack lunches outside to eat on the dusty playground. Never having been around so many kids, everything was new and strange to me, and a little scary. As I wandered around, I noticed some bigger boys playing on the edge of the schoolyard, near a construction site where an addition was being built onto the school. As I approached the older boys, one of them said: "Hey, c'mon, kid, wanna leave your footprint in this wet cement?"

Well, why not? These big kids were doing it, so it must be OK. And wouldn't you know it, just as I finished leaving my footprint for posterity, a teacher caught me in the act and hustled us all off to the principal's office. Terrified, I waited with the big boys in the outer office until the principal could see us. I was thinking dire thoughts—would I be sent home in disgrace on my first day of school, would I be humiliated in front of my classmates? We waited for what seemed an eternity, and were then hustled into the principal's office. There were six or seven boys in the group—I was the only first grader—the others were fifth or sixth graders. After being sternly warned not to do something just because older boys said it was OK, I was sent back to my room.

There would be other trips to the principal's office in later years, but this one was the most memorable. How many kids get sent to the principal's office on their very first day of school? After this

auspicious beginning, the rest of my first year of
school was ho-hum.

13.

***"Eighter from Decatur, County Seat of Wise,
Home of the bedbugs, 'skeeters and the flies."***

An old Wise County Saying

Two weeks after school was out, in June 1943, Dad drove us to the El Paso railroad station taking my mother, Jerry and me to catch the train to Ft. Worth. We were headed back to God's Country, to spend the summer with our grandparents. The train was hot, jammed with soldiers on leave from basic training at Ft. Bliss before being shipped overseas. The trip seemed endless. Squeezed into a hot seat that stuck to my clothes, with men in uniform crowded in the aisles, I could not move around. A cowboy about to enter second grade has got to gallop up and down the aisles, hang out with the army guys smoking Lucky Strikes on the open-air platforms between the cars, go to the front of the train to see the engine, important stuff like that. Fenced in and unable to roam, I was miserable. There were numerous stops along the way, but after Pecos, Odessa, and Midland, I lost track and settled into a heat-induced stupor. We ate homemade pimento cheese sandwiches and apricot fried pies that Mom had packed in a shoe box; I was thirsty the whole trip. I guess Jerry, now two-and-a-half, was miserable too, but had the good grace not to cry too much.

Many hours later, in the middle of the night, our tired little party finally arrived at the Ft. Worth train station. Groggy, I could barely greet the Gage welcoming party. My Aunt Roberta collected me from my mom, who struggled down the steep railroad car steps with a sleeping Jerry over one shoulder and a heavy suitcase in her other hand.

"My goodness, Jimmy Allen, you've grown so much I'm not sure I can carry you," my Aunt said as she draped me over her shoulder. Looking up from Roberta's shoulder as we left the train platform, I noticed my Grandfather Merlin behind us, leaning heavily on a cane as he walked. His 6' 3" frame had shrunk, and he moved slowly and carefully, as if something inside was about to break.

The next morning, I awoke in a strange place, one I had never seen before. It had been less than a year since we left North Texas, but there had been lots of changes. My grandparents no longer lived on the family farm, having sold out and moved to Decatur a few months earlier due to my Grandfather's ill health. He could no longer work the farm.

There would be no hunting with Papa this summer. He hunted in the fall and winter months; summers were too hot and he was too busy farming his Denton County farm. I didn't know it at the time, but I had already been on my last hunt with him.

There were, however, some good times on the Reding family farm that summer, mostly revolving around me shadowing my grandfather as he went about the farming activities. There were horses, chickens and hogs to feed, dogs to train and care for, fields to plow, plant and cultivate. I tried to do it all, or as much as was allowed. I'm sure I was an itch, in the way lots of times, but Hey! I was six going on seven, so gimme a break! Caleb never seemed to mind, but his gruff manner came through at times, and once it was kinda funny—at least he got a laugh out of it.

Papa was harrowing a field in preparation for planting, and as usual I was riding along, now perched on a bale of peanut hay on the harrow behind him and his team of horses, Doc and John. As he made the turn at the end of a row, he stopped the team under the shade of a Hackberry tree, rolled a smoke from his can of Prince Albert, smoked it, then cut a plug of Brown Mule Chewing Tobacco, put it in his cheek, and began smacking away.

I was now sitting beside him in the shade, observing this habitual behavior close at hand. While working I had rarely seen my grandfather without a roll-your-own or a plug of Brown Mule, sometimes both.

"Papa, what's that in your mouth?" I had often wondered, and was now old enough to ask. He always made it seem delicious.

"That's my brown candy, Son, wanna bite?"

I nodded a tentative yes.

"OK," he said, "here's whatcha' do," as he cut off a tiny plug and handed it to me. "Put it in your mouth an' chew it up real good, don't spit it out, swaller it down."

"OK" I thought, and put the brown candy in my mouth, began chewing it up as directed, as he gently turned the team and began moving down the next row. It tasted awful, bitter, not sweet at all, but I chewed it up and swallowed.

Papa got to the end of the row, turned the team around, saw he had lost his harrow rider.

After the swallow I felt sick, got dizzy and fell off the harrow in the middle of the row. There I lay in the hot afternoon sun, not feeling well enough to get up. Having been pretty sure of what would happen, Papa had a good laugh, and drove the team down to pick me up. No more brown candy for me—I never tried chewing tobacco again. Guess aversive conditioning works; it sure did for me.

14.

***To tell the story . . . is to let the place itself
speak through the telling.***

David Abrams, *Places of the Wild*

During that summer of 1943, my father was transferred to an isolated EPNG pumping station located in the desert 100 miles east of El Paso. It was the middle of nowhere, a remote enclave where yucca, creosote bush, mesquite and sotol dotted the rugged desert landscape. Located at the foot of the Guadeloupe Mountains, with the jazzy gas company name of "Number Two", the camp had been built for about thirty or forty company employees and their families. I loved it.

I loved it for a lot of reasons. It was out in the country, way out, away from the crowded confines of El Paso life, where I could roam out into the arroyos, dry washes and mesas that surrounded our little desert oasis. The nearest neighbors lived miles away on huge sheep ranches.

Until we moved to El Paso, I had always been able to roam around the fields and countryside near whatever rural place we lived. Buster and I went on many excursions into unexplored territory. My canine partner wasn't with me anymore, but there were some two-legged pals who were OK substitutes. We explored interesting places, made a fort out of scraps and desert detritus—no girls allowed—and had great fun discovering all the desert critters who lived there. My life-long love of the desert and desert places began here at Number Two.

I liked our two-room school, a far cry from the overcrowded one in first grade, and thought my second grade teacher, Mrs. Pool, was great. Her husband also worked for the gas company, and they lived across the street from us. She often called on me to read in class, and since I was a pretty good reader by then, I began to feel I was her pet; well, one of them anyhow. There were two or three girls who got to do stuff, too, like ring the bell at recess and dust the erasers after school. But I felt I had the inside track, until one fateful day just before Halloween when we had been playing hard during morning recess and I drank a lot of water to cool off.

We were doing math problems on the blackboard when I felt the urge. I sidled over to Mrs. Pool and asked her if I could go to the bathroom. Maybe she was distracted, or just didn't hear me. Anyway, what she said was, "It's just a few minutes 'til lunch time, Jimmy, I think you can wait."

Well, I couldn't wait. I made it back to my seat, crossing my legs and squirming in misery. Finally, unable to hold it back, I felt the warm, wet dribble go down the front of my pants, into my seat, and then saw it begin to pool onto the floor beside my desk. I sat there, too mortified to move, wanting to become invisible---to become tiny, an ant maybe, anything but the embarrassed, wet boy I was, hoping no classmate would see the telltale puddle on the floor. Thankfully no one did, and a few minutes later we were dismissed for lunch. I sprang from my desk and raced to the door, knowing everyone in my class now saw the dark stains on my clothes, knew I had peed my pants and were sniggering at me behind my back. Racing home, I vowed never to go back to that second grade classroom.

Taking pity on me, my mom let me stay home that afternoon. She made Toll House cookies, a favorite treat, and read to Jerry and me until we both fell asleep on the living room couch, the shades pulled to dim the room and shut out the world for a time.

That evening, Mom went across the street to tell Mrs. Pool what happened. Of course, seeing a puddle on the floor and me absent that afternoon, she had figured it out. A few minutes later, both women walked out the Pools' front door and came over to ours. Mrs. Pool was apologetic, saying she was very sorry for my embarrassment, that she should have let me go to the bathroom. I forgave her, almost, but she slipped down a notch on my Favorite Persons list. When I went to school the next day and found no one saying anything about my accident, relief swept through me. In later years, as a teacher, there was never a time when I refused to let a student go to the bathroom when they asked to go, even when I suspected it wasn't because they had to go.

Some people who haven't spent time in desert places think nothing lives there. How wrong they are! The desert is teeming with many different species of life. My friends and I were constantly finding horny toads, lizards, mice, spiders, and all kinds of insects. We were also warned to keep on the lookout for rattlesnakes. My father spoke of desert rattlers that made their way into gas company buildings and sheds at night in search of warmth. Once he brought home a quart jar filled with rattles from snakes his fellow employees had killed. There must have been dozens of rattles of varying sizes in that jar. I was impressed.

But nothing could keep us from playing in and exploring the desert terrain around the company compound. One Saturday, a group of five or six of us boys were playing at our fort, situated about 200 yards beyond the fenced-in area that defined the gas company property. We had just finished putting an old piece of tin on the roof and were feeling pretty satisfied that we now had a roof over part of our fort. Soon realizing that the mid-day heat generated by the tin roof rendered it too hot to sit under, we went in search of a cooler, shady spot to eat the picnic lunches we had brought. We headed single file for a shallow arroyo not far away where a cluster of yuccas provided some shade. Approaching the shaded spot, an older boy who was in the lead heard the unmistakable rattling sound of a rattlesnake. He froze in his tracks, causing the rest of us to do the same.

Spotting the rattler coiled under the shade of a large yucca about twenty feet away, someone said, "Let's kill it," triggering a frantic search for sticks and rocks to use as weapons. Fortunately for us, the snake having ideas other than a confrontation, uncoiled and slithered away. Our brave party followed from a safe distance, watching as the desert rattler swiftly slithered into some rocks further down the arroyo and disappeared. So much for a picnic lunch under yucca shade. Jittery now, we huddled around, everyone talking at once about our encounter with the rattler.

"Wow, didja see how he was coiled up, just like a rope!"

"His rattlers were really loud! I heard him way back there."

"He musta been four feet long!"

"Naw, he was a little'un, only 'bout three feet." This from an older boy of about ten, a seasoned rattlesnake hunter.

By the time we finished discussing the snake's traits, size and speed, he was easily six feet long, and sped away fast as a runaway freight train. Then a kid asked, "What if one of us had been bitten, what would we do?" Then we all pooled our ignorance and came up with a plan. We would make a stretcher by threading a pair of yucca poles through the sleeves of two or three coats, put the bitten kid on the stretcher, and carry him as fast as possible to the sanctuary of the gas company camp, yelling for help all the way. Then another kid said, "OK, let's do it, it'll be fun to see what happens!"

I don't remember how a close encounter with a rattlesnake evolved into a snakebite prank with me as the star victim. What I do remember is this: we made our stretcher out of coats and yucca poles, I got volunteered to be the snakebite victim—complete with fake tourniquet on my leg—was placed on the stretcher, and off the group trotted toward the housing development with me lying on the stretcher, everyone yelling a variation of the theme: "Help, somebody help, Jimmy's been snakebit!"

By the time our band of desert thespians neared the boundary fence, an adult saw us, heard our yells, and came rushing to our rescue. It was my mother.

As luck would have it, our house was one of the closest to where we were playing, and Mom had been standing at the kitchen sink washing lunchtime dishes when she looked out the window over the sink, heard our yells, and came to my aid.

Boy, did she come! If the Olympics had not been canceled because of World War II, my mom could have qualified for the women's 100 meter dash, easy! She was flying like the wind, apron flapping over her housedress, carrying a dish towel like a baton. When the guys saw her reaction to their prank, I was unceremoniously dumped from my perch on the stretcher. Why? They were laughing so hard at my mom streaking toward us, I was forgotten. I had to admit it was pretty funny seeing my mom's record-breaking run to the boundary fence. By the time she got to the fence she was out-of-breath, red of face, and not a happy camper. Realizing it had been a joke, a cruel one, played at her expense, Mom was both relieved and angry. She scolded all of us, then yanked me through the fence, and whapped me with the wet dish towel as I was prodded toward the house. I still think the prank was pretty funny, and the spanking I got that day was worth it.   For some reason, my mom never thought it was that funny.

15.

Expose a child to a particular environment at his susceptible time
And he will perceive in the shapes of that environment until he dies.

Wallace Stegner, *Wolf Willow*

Cowboys and Sheepmen

Every boy I knew who grew up in Texas when I did loved cowboys and wanted to be one. The celluloid world of Gene Autry, Roy Rogers and the Durango Kid figured prominently in my Saturday afternoons in later childhood. My favorite Sunday Comics and comic book hero was Red Ryder, drawn for almost 40 years by Fred Harmon, who lived in Pagosa Springs, Colorado. For years, Red Ryder comic books were among my prized possessions, kept in a cardboard box under my bed. Harmon's beautifully drawn scenery of Southwest Colorado was as appealing to me as were the characters. One memorable Sunday comic strip was a single half-page scene of Red and his sidekick, Little Beaver, towing a Christmas tree on horseback through knee-deep snow to the ranch house, the San Juan Mountains in the background.

My love of Southwest Colorado and Northern New Mexico has it's origins in those comics. In the spring of 1969, I went to Colorado for the first time to interview for a job at Ft. Lewis College in Durango. I remember stepping off the Frontier Airlines plane at La Plata County Airport, pausing on the tarmac, turning to gaze in wonder at the snow-clad San Juan Mountains, thinking, *This is the place I want to be!*

Radio dramas, mysteries and adventures had been an entertainment mainstay in our home for as long as I could remember. During the day, Mom would listen to her soap operas: *Stella Dallas, Backstage Wife* and *Young Doctor Malone*, to name a few. On Saturday and Sunday evenings my ears would be glued to our big Zenith radio in the living room, listening to family shows such as *Suspense, The Shadow, Lux Radio Theater* and *I Love a Mystery*.

On most weekday afternoons around suppertime, I would tear myself away from my outdoor adventures long enough to listen to the children's shows. I heard them all: *Jack Armstrong, Captain Midnight, The Lone Ranger* and my favorite at the time, *Tom Mix*. He came on every day for a fifteen-minute serial, escaping from one close call after another, his Wonder Horse, Tony, figuring prominently in many of them. The hook was, you had to listen every day or you couldn't follow the story line. And I was hooked. The sponsor of the show, Post Grape Nut Flakes, is still my favorite cereal.

I thrilled to the narrow escapes, the more improbable the better, and laughed at the antics of his sidekick, "Wash". I identified with Tom on many levels, but mainly because he was a cowboy, and so was I. My playmates and I spent many hours acting out a cowboy's adventurous life. There was a difference, however, between my friends and me— they were *pretending* to be cowboys; I *was* a cowboy!

My vision of who a cowboy was and what he looked like got a heavy dose of reality not long after the rattlesnake incident. We had been forbidden to go out in the desert, at least for now, and had to be content to play within the perimeter of the gas company boundary fence. We didn't like it much, but what were we to do? We decided to build another fort, so began to collect building materials, constructing it as close as possible to the boundary fence and our old fort.

One afternoon after school, adding to the new and woefully inadequate structure, daydreaming about the adventures waiting just over the fence, I noticed a rider on horseback slowly moving down the fence line some distance away. As he neared, his features more distinct now, I gaped at this real-life apparition. The hat he wore had a tall crown, creased like the one Tom Mix wore, but here any similarity between him and my radio cowboy ceased. This horseman looked nothing like my comic book or radio heroes. When new, his hat must have been black, but faded now, worn, discolored by sweat and sun, it was several shades of dusty gray, the broad brim turned down in front, shading the man's eyes. The only exposed part of his body was his lower jaw and chin, sun-browned, unshaven and grizzled. He sat slouched in the saddle, looking weary. As his slow-moving horse drew up opposite me, he "woahed" the bony bay, grinned down at me and spoke: "Howdy, son, how y'all doin'?"

Ray and Jimmy Davis, who were also working on the fort, walked up beside me, struck dumb by this real-life cowboy on horseback. I edged closer to the fence, eyes devouring every detail. A wide, leather belt clasped a sheathed, long-bladed knife on his left hip, but no holstered revolver on his right. A scabbarded rifle angled backward on this side of the saddle. I then noticed a gun-belt draped over the saddle horn, a gun, *not* a western revolver, in the holster. My cowboy images were becoming scrambled.

The shirt he wore was faded to an indeterminate color, grease-and sweat-stained, buttoned up to the top button. His dirty, faded jeans were tucked into the tops of tall, stovepipe, flat-heeled boots with rounded toes. A pair of Spanish spurs completed his outfit, large rowels jingling as the horse shifted position.

Trying to recall my long-ago memory of this cowboy, a more recent image comes to mind, one from a favorite western novel, *Monte Walsh* by Owen Wister, perhaps the best ever at portraying the real life of a cowboy. Made into an unforgettable movie starring Lee Marvin and Jack Palance, a character from that film is almost identical to my 1940's cowboy—a grizzled old cowboy, bony and slender, crazed by his years of line-riding solitude, gallops away down a steep mesa, on his way to an inevitable end. "He's chasin' his last cow," says Monte.

This horseman sat there in comfortable silence for a few moments, pulled a boot out of the off-side stirrup and slowly draped his leg over the saddle horn, side-saddle style, spur rowel sounding a pleasant tinkle. He reached for the large canteen slung over the pommel of the saddle, drank deeply, then sloshed it around and muttered, "Bout out. Don't suppose you boys could spare a little drinkin' water?"

Did we have drinking water! We could give him all the water he wanted. Scurrying to meet his request, the other Jimmy grabbed the canteen and ran off to fill it.

Waiting for the canteen to be filled, I inched closer, pushing up against the fence, near enough to reach out and pet his horse's muzzle. The familiar horse smell mingled with others: leather, tobacco, body odor, creosote, sagebrush, and a vaguely familiar, feral animal scent now stronger than the others. The cowboy withdrew a tin of Prince Albert from a shirt pocket and began to roll a smoke the same way I had seen Papa do countless times. Same kind of tobacco, too. As he sifted tobacco into the creased cigarette paper, the horse shifted and snorted, causing the man to lose the loose shreds.

"Whoa, you jughead." Tapping the can again, he finished rolling his smoke.

Something clanked on the far side of the saddle. Catching a glimpse of curved metal with jagged edges, something clicked, and I now recognized the powerful astringent animal smell. The clanking noise was animal traps, the feral smell was wolf or coyote bait, made from the animal's urine.

Neuroscientists tell us that the sense of smell is the sense we retain the longest and triggers the clearest memories. One whiff of this potent perfume and I was immediately transported to an earlier time and place.

An individual life passes through a continuum of time and space, but now and then you enter a warp that sucks you back into the past: I am four years old, almost five, but still too young according to my mother, to go hunting with Papa, which is my benchmark for maturity these days. I am allowed, however, to shadow him around on all other outings, and this morning we are headed to the general store in Roanoke, a few miles west of the Ray Foreman place, which my grandparents now farm in southern Denton County.

It is springtime, everything is in fragrant bloom. April can be a glorious time in Texas. I am riding shotgun in my grandfather's Model A pickup, window down, warm breeze blowing my face as I lean out the window, spring fragrances mingling with newly-mown hay, harness leather and Papa's tobacco into a hypnotic mix. I am in "hog heaven".

We are going to pick up a part needed to repair the seed drill, which broke this morning as Papa was planting corn. As usual when I am here, I was riding beside him, sitting on a sack of seed corn placed there for my comfort. Earlier, we had planted only a few rows when the drill gears made a snapping sound, the wheels locked, and the team of horses pulling the drill was jerked to a stop. Papa shouted out a few well-chosen invectives, lets fly a stream of tobacco juice, then hopped down from the seat and slammed open the long, rectangular box holding the seed corn. From my exalted perch I saw him plunge both arms down into the corn, feel around the bottom of the planter box for a few moments, then pulled out a broken gear the size of a half-dollar.

"I hope they have one of these in Roanoke," he said, peering suspiciously at the broken part. In all things animal or organic—dogs, horses, people, soil, the countryside—my grandfather is confident, patient, knowing. But things mechanical are different; they're supposed to work, not break down, and when they do—which is often on his marginal farming operation—patience and confidence often fly out the window.

"I'm a farmer, not no dam' mechanic," I heard him say on more than one occasion after a mechanical breakdown.

Traveling toward Roanoke, hand airplaning in the breeze, I am imagining the jars of penny candy on the shelves at the front of the store. How many pieces can I buy with this nickel clutched in my sweaty palm? A Tom's peanut butter log, some salt water taffy, maybe a Pinkerton's Peanut Patty—I'm partial to anything with peanuts in it. My grandfather also grows a few acres of peanuts on this sandy loam farm. No real money in raising peanuts on this small scale, but peanut hay is a horse's favorite, and high in protein.

As we begin to turn a corner on the tree-lined, unpaved sand and gravel two-lane road, a sedan pulls up close behind us, driver eager to pass. Papa looks in the side view mirror, sees the car and hunkers forward, both hands now clutching the steering wheel. Rounding the corner onto a stretch of straight road, the sedan starts to pass,_Papa hunches further over the steering wheel, throwing nervous glances at the passing car, his two-handed death grip over-steering the Model A. Fishtailing now in the sandy lane, we slow down to a crawl, Papa shifting up into second gear. I notice beads of sweat on the backs of his rough, brown hands. He drives a team of horses much better than this jitney.

At the Roanoke Store, we pull in beside a black sedan that looks like the one that passed us. As we get out of the pickup, Papa glares inside the suspicious vehicle, then looks around the parking area at the other dusty farm trucks. But the driver, probably an escapee from the Denton County Jail, is nowhere to be seen. Maybe he's inside, holding up the place.   I step up on the running board, peer inside. Looks OK to me.

We move toward the feed store entrance, up side steps to the dock, then through a double door used to load feed and other farm supplies. It is dark inside after the bright sunlight, and we stand just inside the door, waiting for our eyes to adjust to the dim light. The air inside is warm, rich, sweet, mingled with familiar smells: sorghum molasses, hay, cottonseed meal, leather. The large room is mazed with tall shelves jammed with items for the farm and farmer. In the middle of the room, toward the back, a window illuminates a pot-bellied stove, cold now, but a magnet nevertheless, for the group of four or five men who sit or stand around it, smoking or chewing, shootin' the breeze. This is a favorite farmer hangout on more leisurely winter days, the men drawn here now out of habit or bad luck, like Papa, here for an item of machinery repair. Never too busy to stop for a few minutes of chit-chat, he moves in that direction, greeting the men gathered there, me trailing behind; he knows them all.

"Hey, Caleb, how yew been? Planted yer corn already? Gone huntin' lately?" With my grandfather's arrival, the talk around the stove turns to hunting, hunting dogs and the availability of game. A Maxwell House Coffee can serves as a communal spittoon, the open grate of the wood stove receives ashes for the roll-your-own smokes.

When the conversation drifts to planting season (ground too wet to plow/too dry to plant), the prospects for rain (not good/too dam' wet), or for a good crop of corn/cotton/peanuts (fair to middlin'), my attention begins to wander. I have roamed these aisles before, peering into this treasure trove of kegs and bins and shelves, surreptitiously gnawing on a piece of cottonseed meal cow cake, a favorite snack, easing into the front part of the store for a bag of penny candy. Papa holds forth near the cold stove, regaling a rapt audience with hunting tales. By now, he has been hunting and raising hunting dogs for almost 50 years. Other hunters listen to what he has to say. He's always good for a story or two.

But today he can't linger, he has a planter to fix, corn to plant. He begins to edge away.

"Gotta go, boys, my dang planter's busted." Papa pulls the broken gear out of his khaki shirt pocket, holding it up as proof.

"Need any help?" This from a mechanically inclined nephew of my grandmother who grins and winks his recognition at me. He is a hunting partner, Shott Myers, who I have seen helping Papa fix a broken harrow. Most of his friends, and all of his hunting buddies, know him to be an impatient and lack-luster mechanic. My grandmother is one of eleven children, so there is often a willing cousin or nephew, a hunting crony, available to help with mechanical repairs. More time for hunting, less wear and tear on the cranky old Master.

"Naw thanks, Shott. Think I kin fix 'er if Walter has 'is drill gear." Nodding, as he says this, toward the owner in the back of the store helping another customer.

"Looks like you brought a new hand with you." This for my benefit. Until now, I have been standing behind my grandfather's right leg, peering around at these springtime slackers, all ears, sponging up what is being said.

"This here's my grandson—Nona and JG's boy." I bask in the glow of the men's attention for a few moments, proud to be Caleb Reding's grandson, too shy to say anything.

Turning, Papa strides toward the back of the store, the heels of his high-topped work boots making a hollow "thud" on the wooden floor as he seeks help to replace the broken part.   I move to a different corner of the store, drawn by a bright light and familiar sounds. Dozens of newly hatched chicks, in various stages of early development, some still wet, are crowded into a large, galvanized oval trough, peeping, moving about under bright incubator lights. I have seen my mother hatching chicks like this in a washtub placed next to the cook stove in our kitchen. They are endlessly fascinating, this new life, so rapidly developing, eager, a brilliant mix of red, brown, yellow, black, white and multi-colored fuzz, peeping, pecking and scratching at food, tiny entrants in a race for life they will not win.

I watch for a while, and just as I'm about to pick up a black one, my grandfather taps me on the back.

"Put 'im down, Son. Let's go." He has found a replacement for the broken gear, wants to get back to the farm, hoping to fix the planter by dinner-time, and heads for the door. This is not looking good; I have a nickel burning a hole in my pocket, so hurry to catch up with his long-legged gait.

"But Papa, Mama gave me a nickel for candy!" At the door now, he turns, looks down at my pitiful face, relents.

"Aw'right, Son, but hurry. We got work to do. Meet me outside." My forlorn look worked! I scurry down the aisle leading to the front of the store, where groceries and candies are sold, again clutching my nickel.

Outside with my bag of sweets, jaws bulging, working on a half-eaten peanut patty, I see Papa leaning over the bed of a rattle-trap pickup even older than his vintage model, talking with a tiny old man whose long, scraggly-gray beard reaches half-way down his shrunken chest. The stranger holds his hunting cap in one hand. He is completely bald, the top of his head a pasty white crown that contrasts with the leathery-brown lower half. He wears greasy, faded overalls tucked into the tops of tall, lace-up hunting boots—the only thing about him I like.

I have seen those same high-topped hunting boots in a Montgomery-Wards Catalog—I want a pair when I'm old enough to go hunting with Papa. In his other hand he holds a pint Mason jar about three-quarters full of a dark yellow liquid. As I approach, the gnome-like man unscrews the lid, passes the open jar to my grandfather who takes a tentative sniff, then draws back with a grimace. The two caged hounds in the bed of the pickup smell the stuff too and react loudly, scrabbling around in the too-small cage, baying mournfully. The little man picks up a vicious-looking animal trap, raps it on the side of the cage, yells, "Shutup!" The dogs cower and are quiet. I now like him even less.

"It's the real McCoy, aw'right." This from Papa as he hands the jar back to the man.

"Jist finished collecting the last of it 'yestidy. It'll git better after awhile." He screws the lid back on the jar. I don't know what's in it, but I catch a slight whiff of something strong and fetid.

"What is it, Papa?"

"Wolf bait, Son, wanna smell?" I'm not sure I do, but nod anyway. I'll try anything Papa does. The jar is handed over again. My grandfather carefully unscrews the lid, passes the open jar under my nose. I inhale.

It is the worst smell of my life, worse even than skunk, which has always been sniffed from a distance, dispersed, not concentrated in a jar like this.

I learn later that the fluid is urine collected from dead coyotes or foxes, allowed to ferment for a few weeks, then sprinkled on traps. I gag, drop my sack of candy in the dust, double over, coughing out my mouthful of candy, almost throw up. A long minute passes. Papa retrieves my candy from the ground tries to wipe it off, but the unwrapped pieces, most of them, are sticky from the warm day and now covered with grit. I'll eat it anyway, but not now. I still feel like I might puke.

"Pretty strong, ain't it, kid?" The gnome is grinning, tobacco-stained teeth a gapped grimace. I hate him. I've never seen my grandfather use traps in his hunting, so I wonder what's up. Papa smiles, too, but there is also a worried look in his eyes, and I think I know where it comes from. If my grandmother finds out he has stuck this foul-smelling stuff under her unsuspecting darling's nose causing such a reaction, there will be hell to pay. I may be Papa's favorite, but I am also my Mama's. Armed with that thought, I feel a little better.

Jerked from my reverie back to the present when the other Jimmy trots up with the filled canteen, I lean against the fence to touch the soft muzzle, the familiar, pleasant horse smell a comfort. The rider leans down, takes the water bottle.

"Thankee kindly, son". Jimmy grins. The rider takes a long drink from the canteen, finishes his smoke, grinds it out on a stirrup, preparing to leave.

I finally work up enough courage to ask: "Have you been trappin' wolves?"

"What you know 'bout trappin' wolves, Son?" A curious grin creases his face.

"My grandfather's a wolf hunter," I say proudly.

"Ain't many wolves in this country now. Them's coyote traps. They git after newborn lambs somethin' fierce." He stands up in the stirrups, straightening the saddle slightly, spurs a-jingle, leather creaking. At this, the horse rears his head, shaking it at the sudden movement, snorts in disgust, teeth chomping on the bit. He is ready to go, too.

"Tell yer dads to bring ya'll over to the ranch in the spring if you'd like to see the sheep shearing. It's a sight if you ain't never seen it." With that invitation he lifts his hand in a goodbye salute and rides away down the fence-line, our eyes locked on him until he disappears over a low hill.

"Boy," the other Jimmy said, "there goes a real cowboy!"

His brother Ray, three years older and worldly wise, corrects him. "He ain't no *cow* boy, he's a sheepman. But he's real, aw'right."

We regale our parents with tales about the line rider, his horse, guns and gear, pestering them until Dad agrees take us to the sheep shearing in the Spring. We are delighted.

Early one Saturday morning in April, my father drove my two friends and me to the sheep ranch headquarters, located about ten miles south of the gas company camp over a rough, unpaved road.

Since my father and both grandparents were farmers who raised cattle, hogs and chickens, I considered myself something of an expert on farm livestock, but I didn't have a clue about what to expect from this sheep-ranching adventure. As we bounced along over what seemed like an endless rocky road, up one draw and down another, my first impression was that the ranch was huge, measured in sections rather than acres, as my grandparents' farms were.

As we approached the ranch headquarters, the size of ranching operations was verified. There was a big adobe ranch house, much like the Mexican hacienda I had seen pictured in one of my readers. Surrounding the ranch house in a large, irregular square were numerous outbuildings, several smaller adobe dwellings, a large bunkhouse and two long, low-roofed barns where the shearing was going on. And there were the sheep, hundreds of them, penned up in enormous corrals, divided as to function. The largest corral held most of the sheep and lambs, where at one end men and sheep dogs were separating the lambs from their mothers, man-handling the lambs into another smaller arena where those separated were bleating, high-pitched and pitiful. Through the fence their mamas were "baaa-ing" a lower-pitched echo. One mama ewe had backed up to the fence, allowing her baby to nurse through the wire. Clouds of dust were everywhere.

Noisy and dusty is mostly how I remember that sheep ranch, and the smell. It was oily, becoming stronger as we parked, got out and walked toward the barn where the sheep were being sheared. The shearing barn was long with a low roof, open on both sides, with small pens along one side so that the sheep were herded into from a long, narrow chute. Along the other side of the barn ran a second large corral where freshly sheared sheep, now white and skeletal, dazed from the double whammy of shearing and vaccinations, staggered around, heads low, tongues lolling out. I was both fascinated and repelled by this strange scenario.

Down the middle of the barn I counted a line of six men in various stages of sheep shearing, all but one using hand-held shears. At the end of the line near the south entrance to the barn, a sixth man was bending down to begin shearing a squirming sheep, wielding a lone pair of electric clippers. He spoke to a group of several onlookers, gesturing with the clippers to make a point unheard at our end of the shed due to the noisy commotion around us. Tall, stooped-shouldered, a handlebar mustache covering half of a two-tone face, he went to work on the sheep, the buzzing clippers slicing the wooly coat off the animal in fat, narrow skeins. The observers crowded around the electric clipper lesson, blocking my view. My eyes shifted to watch one of the other shearers finish clipping a mama ewe as she was boosted to her feet by a nearby helper, a young, barefoot Mexican boy not much bigger than me hustled her, udder full and pendulous, through a gate to join her newly-mown sisters.

As I looked back at the electric sheepman, he stood up, finished, a satisfied grin on his face, and handed the clippers to a nearby onlooker, gesturing for him to try his hand with the new gadget. Noticing us for the first time, he gave a wave and headed our way with a long-legged stride, detouring to grab a wide-brimmed cowboy hat off a nearby gate post. Holding the hat by the brim, he slapped it against one thigh, then the other, each slap sending a cloud of dust off his clothing. He strode toward us, making comments to several of the workers as he wove down the line. As we met and visited with him, we learned that he was the ranch owner, running about 3000 head of sheep and 200 angora goats on 35 sections of land which stretched north and east toward the foothills of the Guadeloupe Mountains. A portion of this ranch became part of Guadeloupe Mountains National Park in 1947.

We were invited to stay for lunch, and after watching the shearing and lamb separation a while longer, we moved over to the outdoor kitchen and eating area for a sample of the food. It was late morning now, hot, with very little breeze. The large *ramada*, which shaded the eating area and cooking center, was covered by yucca poles and a large canvas. We sat under the shade for a while to cool off. A Mexican woman wearing a flour-covered apron brought a tray containing a pitcher filled with iced tea and glasses filled with ice. The tea was sweet and cold—such a treat! I drank my first glass too fast and got a brain freeze! Several women bustled around fire-pits, grills and Dutch ovens, cooking huge amounts of food. The smells were mouth-watering, and our little band of hungry gringos was treated like royalty that day. Very quickly, the table where we sat was loaded down with everything on the menu. There was American food, but I zeroed in on the Mexican food, which was exotic and delicious: tortillas, tamales, enchiladas, mutton stew made with spicy red chilies, frijoles and some kind of sweet bread sprinkled with cinnamon, which I learned in later years were called *bunuelas*. Since moving to El Paso, my mother, an excellent cook, had tried her hand at tacos and enchiladas, but I had never tasted Mexican food like that. My love for Mexican food probably began that day.

It wasn't just the food that was memorable about the meal on this hot day 60 years ago. The whole eating experience was a wonder to me. Just as we began to dig in to the feast on our table, the rancher's wife clanged the dinner bell, and soon men began arriving to wash up at a nearby water trough and line up to be served from tables at the front of the *ramada*, now laden with huge amounts and variety of American and Mexican food. The men, mostly Mexicans, were polite and quiet while in line, but once seated, talked and laughed animatedly, joking and poking fun at each other with familiar ease, all in Spanish. It was a happy meal. I had never seen so many men eat so much food so quickly, or have so much fun while doing it!

Everyone in my dad's car must have gone home that day with a smile on his face. I know I did. I would recall this day on the sheep ranch many times over the years. The earliest good memories stay with us forever. Unfortunately, so do some bad ones.

16.

A few weeks later, near the end of school, I was invited to stay overnight by my friend Billy Townsend, a third-grader, whose family also had a sheep ranch skirting the Guadeloupe Mountains a number of miles to the northeast. This would be my first overnight spent away from my family—staying with grandparents doesn't count. This was exciting enough, but the prospect of again visiting ranching operations which had so fascinated me, with the added bonus of going horseback riding in the mountains, sent me into fits of delirium. While I had been around horses all my life, and had ridden several, the prospect of actually riding a horse on mountain trails was thrilling.

The day of the big weekend arrived, and I could hardly wait for school to be out that Friday afternoon in early May. Finally, Billy and I raced to our house after school, waiting impatiently for his mother to pick us up.

Memories of that weekend spent on the Townsend Ranch are scant but vivid.

The ride to the ranch bounced over the rough ranch road for several miles, the pickup gaining altitude toward a jagged mountain reflecting ochre and chocolate in the afternoon sun. Ranch headquarters were nestled in a shallow valley at the base of the stark mountain. The ranch house was situated on a high point of land, overlooking barns, bunkhouses and outbuildings. From the front porch a panoramic view stretched north to the mountains, south and east toward the desert floor and beyond to a ridge of mesas and distant peaks.

But what does a seven-year-old care for panorama? I was interested in horses! After stowing the paper sack filled with my belongings on the bunk bed where I was to sleep, we raced down to the horse corral, where Billy's dad had bridled horses waiting. Billy had his own horse; I was given a gentle old nag that wouldn't go faster than a rough trot—such is the plight of a fledgling cowboy. I earned points with his father by demonstrating I could saddle my own horse, then promptly lost them when I got on the horse, dropped a bridle rein, and needed help retrieving it. After tying a knot in my reins, we trotted off with orders to be back before sundown. My friend showed me his favorite places: caves large enough to stand up in, with feral smells and animal bones, a tiny waterfall that threaded down a sheer cliff into a secret pool several feet deep—deep enough to paddle around in, cold and clear and delicious. Around the pool, Billy pointed out deer tracks and those of some predator, perhaps mountain lion or bobcat. On the ride back to the ranch house we saw white dots high up on the ridges—desert mountain sheep. The mountains had all these wonders, and more. They still do.

The next day, Saturday, I indulged my cowboy fantasies to the fullest. I tried my hand at roping a calf (Billy was good; I couldn't get the hang of it). We rode again to his favorite spots; took turns being hero and villain, killing each other a dozen times over, inventing new and dramatic ways of dying: falling out of the loft into a pile of hay, off fences, even into the water trough in the horse corral which got us marched up to the ranch house, soaking wet, for dry clothes.

The other memories of that weekend on the ranch are from that evening, following our day of western adventures. After supper, tired, content and happy, I sat with the family on the front porch as dusk moved to evening, listening to Saturday night radio shows: *I Love a Mystery* and *The Creaking Door*, both scary enough to send shivers down my spine. The chill mountain air (ranch headquarters was above 5,000 feet) had me reaching for a blanket. Moving to the front steps, I noticed an orange streak tracking across the sky. I had seen shooting stars before, but nothing like this one.

"Look at that falling star!" I exclaimed, everyone turning to see where I pointed.

"Wow, it's really close!" as it continued its downward streak. A few moments later it plunged to earth on the desert floor several miles away. There was an orange fireball, followed by a dull "thud", followed by what sounded like firecrackers.

"That ain't no fallin' star," Mr. Townsend said, a tinge of fear in his voice.

The smell of burned human flesh is one that stays with you always. It never goes away.

J.D. Salinger, *The Catcher in the Rye.*

The following week we learned that a B-17 bomber on a training mission from Ft. Bliss in El Paso had caught fire in mid-air and crashed with a crew of nine. No survivors. As my second year of school drew to an end, Tojo's War finally intruded into my life. On the Saturday before school let out for the summer, a group of us rode in the Davis' old flat-bed truck, lurching over a rough path through the desert to the bomber disaster. Morbid curiosity gets us all. Topping a rise, the crash site now visible, there was little to indicate it had ever been an airplane. Charred wreckage was scattered around a blackened area in the rocky landscape. As we drew nearer, the remains of a metal seat, part of the instrument panel and a small tail section were all that was recognizable. Lurching to a stop, we piled out of the truck, slowly scattering around the wreckage.

No longer eager, I held back, noticed dark clouds to the north, threatening a May thunderstorm. A cool wind carried moisture, the scent of desert plants, and others— stronger, not of the desert--- burned metal, similar to smells around a blacksmith's forge, and another; this one, more dense, unforgettable, a smell which remains seared in my memory. Burned human flesh smells like nothing else: sickly sweet, coppery, horrific.

It was a smell all must have identified, but no one talked about. No one talked at all. We had come to this now sacred place, intruders at a funeral pyre, and embarrassed, kept silent lest we say something stupid or uncaring. The scent of burned flesh blocked out my other senses. I wandered around a few minutes, then headed back to the truck, ready to leave.

A few minutes later, the rest of our group was ready go, and still silent, crowded back into the truck. My father and I rode standing up in the truck bed, the wind now at our backs, a strong whiff of rain on sagebrush and creosote helping to clear my head of the darker smells. I turned to look back one last time before we lost sight of the crash scene. The clouds were lower now, obscuring the mountains, a strong north wind pushing us away from this dark spot. It was a silent ride home.

17.

<u>**The journey continues . . .**</u>

My destination on this day is Van Horn, about a hundred miles east of El Paso and gateway to the Guadeloupe Mountains. This little West Texas town is a familiar stop. During a five year period in the 1980's we lived in the Davis Mountains/Big Bend Country near Alpine, 120 miles south of here. About once a month, Susan and I would load the kids into the camper of Old Goldy, my 1970 Chevy pickup, and head for El Paso for an escape weekend of shopping, dining out and a movie. On many of these trips we stayed at the El Presidente, our favorite hotel in the border town of Juarez, and while there shopped at the large Saturday Market and ate at two or three of our favorite Mexico restaurants. Van Horn, being about halfway, was our usual stopping place for gas and potty breaks.

Almost there, I notice a road sign, "Van Horn 18 miles; El Paso 138 miles." As the freeway begins a gradual decent into a wide, shallow bowl I see a familiar natural phenomenon in the distance: strong westerly winds swoop over and down the rusty-brown mountain foothills, creating a dust cloud which now obscures the sun. I count four muscular dust devils, miniature tornadoes shouldering sand, desert debris, and in one a glitter of trash, into swirling dances, zigging and zagging to tunes only they can hear.

Having forgotten I am about to pass over into Mountain Standard Time, I realize it will be just 4 P.M., too early to stop for the night. The days are getting a little longer, there's plenty of daylight left, so decide to continue on north, toward the mountains. I fill the gas tank, grab a couple of barbecue sandwiches and wheel the little red Capri northward toward the Guadeloupes, now about 50 miles away. Halfway through my first sandwich I feel a crunch, then bite down on something hard. What is it?

The state highway is narrow, winding and rough, so I look for a place to pull over. After about two miles I find a turnoff to a ranch, pull over, and look at the bite of barbecue in my hand. Dang! The crunch I felt was my bridge breaking off. I now have one exposed tooth, ground down to the pulp, one broken tooth, and a gap where the crown filled a missing molar. There won't be much solid food eaten until I can get to my dentist in Farmington. There's no pain, but the exposed teeth feel raw and tender.

Frustrated, I scissor myself out of the little car, and as I do so feel the return of that pain in my lower back. It is sharper now, and feel the need to loosen my body up, so try to touch my toes and do slow upper torso rotations. This helps a little, but my back still hurts, so I walk up the gravel road to the closed ranch gate, lean my forearms over the top of the gate and look around, reminding myself that I *have* been on the road nonstop for 400 miles.

Rusty red desert mountains and tall mesas dotted with yucca, mesquite and creosote, surround me. The ranch road trails off for several miles to the east before disappearing over a low mesa. There is no ranch house or outbuildings in sight. I turn, do a slow 360, looking for signs of human habitation. Except for the ranch road and another one to the northwest winding around the base of a high mesa, its white chalk track vanishing around cinnamon brown outcrops, there are no signs of people, no traffic on this secondary highway.

The silence is profound. It is very still, no breeze, a sure sign that dusk is approaching in this country where wind is a constant companion. When we lived near Alpine, in a beautiful, secluded spot in the Davis Mountains a few miles west of town, the only time you could count on the wind not blowing was either at dawn or dusk. The rest of the time it blew, always. If we still lived there, I would erect a wind generator to provide renewable energy. Here in this part of West Texas, the wind is an abundant energy source, cheap, renewable and constant.

This rugged Chihuahuan Desert country, remote, with few people, is country I love as only one who discovers the desert at an early age can, before greener places leave their indelible marks on the psyche. When we moved near here 60 years ago, it was love at first sight. Freed from the unfamiliar, crowded restrictions of war-time El Paso, that seven-year-old boy was able to escape into these foothills and arroyos, able to roam at will in what became his special wilderness landscape.

Standing here, enveloped by the cool dryness of this end-of-winter arid spot, the late afternoon sun is just touching the western peaks. I breathe deeply, now smelling the distinct desert flora, enjoying the faint but pungent mixture of creosote bush, sagebrush, sotol, prickly pear and chamisa. I love this country as only a native can.

If I'm going to find the spot where EPNG Station Number Two is, or was, located, I need to go. Folded back into the car, I arrow toward the desert peaks. The highest mountain in Texas at just over 8,000 feet, Guadeloupe Peak, looms ahead, its shear, southern face is now burnt orange, the rays of the setting sun striking straight on, blazing fire from its steep cliff.

Riding on, tired now in this small saddle, the stiff sports car suspension does little to lessen the jolts over the rough asphalt. I'm ready to end this driving marathon.

A few miles south of the junction of U.S. 180/67 I get visual confirmation of my earlier musings about the wind generator as a wise choice for clean, renewable energy. On the darkening eastern horizon, spread out for miles in an irregular line, I see dozens of industrial strength wind turbines, some slowly turning, some still. A utility company somewhere is generating renewable energy for thousands of lucky customers.

I come to the highway intersection, and pause, wondering which way to turn. The map shows the road to the right curving north into Guadeloupe Mountains National Park; to the left it is a straight shot west for a hundred miles to El Paso. I guess left, and after traveling less than a mile beyond the intersection, spot a structure that triggers a memory. On the right is a long-abandoned gas station and café, vaguely familiar, the wooden canopy jutting out to cover phantom gas pumps. Braking quickly, I wheel the sportster off the blacktop onto the hard-packed, chalk-like caliche gravel at the front of the station, pull under the overhang and get out. Yes, this feels right. Memories flood back.

I am remembering my dad pulling our 1936 Chevrolet under this very overhang, where we would stop for gas and a few essentials all those years ago. I begin to wander around, peering into the streaked windows of the gas station/store/café, looking for something familiar. There was no café here back then, only a place to buy gas and a few groceries, grandfather to today's gas and convenience stores.

On the west side of the building, a large hole was dug for a mechanic to work underneath cars by running the vehicle onto heavy, wooden ground-level planks. The supporting timbers are now bleached almost white by the relentless desert sun, decaying, near collapse. In today's world, hydraulics raise and lower autos for convenient access. This cinches it: this is the gas station out of my past. The location of EPNG # 2 is nearby.

As I continue to wander around, trying to fit this place into the slot reserved for it in my memory, I glance across the highway and notice a stand of tall evergreens which shade the west side of a house and outbuildings, neat and orderly, out of place stuck out here in the middle of nowhere. No familiarity there, these interlopers on my childhood turf. A tall man in a blue baseball cap is watering something in his front yard and eyeing me suspiciously. There's nothing around here to steal, so what is he worried about?

Continuing to look around and strolling around behind the building, I notice an automated natural gas pumping station about two hundred yards away. Returning to the car, I begin writing some notes in my journal when I hear the crunch of gravel under slow-moving tires. I look up to see Blue Cap now in a tall van, stopped near enough for me to read the stitching on his cap: "Port Townsend, Washington", and on the bill: "USN".   Retired Navy. The ship/shape place across the road makes sense now—a spit-and-polish guy.

"Can I help you?"

"I hope so. There used to be an El Paso Gas Company Station around here, houses, a school. Do you know anything about it?"

"Yeah, it was right there," indicating with a slight lift of his chin toward the natural gas apparatus I noticed a minute ago. I can't see his hands; maybe he's holding a Navy Colt on his lap. The Navajo-style chin-point he gives me is one I have seen often over the years in Indian Country. I stifle a grin. I love Navajos' dry sense of humor; they poke fun at everyone, particularly themselves, and I have heard jokes and songs about this minimalist style of Indian communication.   Chin-pointing, lip-pursing, eyes-moving—all have subtle meanings, and I once heard a Navajo storyteller bring an audience to tears of laughter with a ribald tale about a Navajo sheepherder giving directions to a lost "Belegana" (English translation: stinking white-eyes).

But I am still doubtful about this place. My childhood memories have the location on the south side of the highway, not on the north as indicated by the chin point. Thanking him, hoping to break the ice for more information, I tell him my family lived here for a time during the war; that I am trying to retrace some old steps. He looks me up and down, maybe moving me down a notch on his Suspects List from arsonist/terrorist to nutty old fart on a fool's mission. He nods, and after a long pause, says, "They automated the station about twelve years ago. Used to be about 30 houses over there." Another chin-pointing.

Loquacious now, he tells me the schoolhouse was moved to a nearby ranch, and that triggers a memory. About ten miles back down the state highway to Van Horn, I saw a sign at the entrance to a distant ranch: "Summerfield School." Maybe that was it, the school I attended during second grade. I'll have to check. I ask him if he owns this property, indicating with a sweep of my arm the gas station/store.

"Yeah," he says, and I now peg him as just a suspicious property owner. I don't blame him. If I saw a geezer in faded overalls snooping around, I'd be suspicious too. (I could be a terrorist; have often had Monkey Wrenching tendencies, *heh, heh, heh.*)

This is all he's going to tell me, so I thank him and move toward the car. Before I climb in, I turn for a final look around. The sun has set now, the western sky is a dark crimson, tailing off on bruised purple fingers clawing for a grip in the westering jet stream. You can't beat a western sunset when there's dust in the air.

Below the horizon I can see what looks like a frozen lake, white and smooth, stretching north to south for miles: Salt Flats. Though not as large or well-known as the salt flats in Utah, people have been known to race vehicles along its length. Automobile commercials have been made here.

Before heading for El Paso, there is one last stop I must make. Wheeling the car around the chalky gravel, I drive up the shoulder of U.S. 180 for about 50 yards, make a right turn across a cattle guard, noting a sign marking gas company property. Continuing slowly for a couple hundred yards, approaching the intricate structure of the natural gas station, I look for any familiar landmark that might jog my memory, but nothing looks like anything I remember. I stop in what could have been the middle of the housing area, get out, looking around for anything recognizable, but all these years later any trace of the familiar has been cleared away. Nothing remains except some disturbed earth, small desert plants barely surviving, and a shallow curb covered completely in places by the caliche gravel. I have a vague memory of a curb like this lining the gravel street where we lived, marking the division between the street and the narrow property on which the houses sat, most of them two-bedroom, asbestos-shingled duplexes.

But in that long-ago memory, the orientation of this whole place is 180 degrees out of kilter. I remember Number Two being on the other side of the road, not here on the north side, and the mountains were farther away, the desert was not this desolate. Did they move everything over here without telling me? But no, Navy Blue Cap said it was right here, where I'm standing. I begin to quarter the area, moving in larger and larger circles, looking for anything else I might recognize, but it's no use. So much for the accuracy of childhood memories.

This must be the place, but no human landmarks remain; only the mountains and desert landscape remind me that I lived, was schooled, and played here a long time ago. Like a wise man once said, "If you want to know what kind of lasting impression you make, stick your finger in a glass of water, then pull it out."

Out on U.S. 180 a couple hundred yards away, cars and trucks whiz by, lights on now in the gathering dusk, their drivers unaware of the dramas and dreams played out over the years by those of us no longer here. There are no lasting human imprints marking this place, but there are indelible childhood memories, and that's enough.

When I was seven years old we moved to this remote spot, and I remember it with fondness as a place where my mates and I played out great adventures, encountered two-legged, four legged, and no-legged desert dwellers, rode horses imaginary and real, killed villains, learned some hard lessons about life. Are these memories real, or just a fantasy? I'll take a good fantasy to most of today's reality.

Almost dark now, only a faint orange glow outlines the inky horizon. Driving slowly out toward the highway, tires crunching on the sun-bleached caliche, I stop to ponder my options beside the company sign I can just make out in the fading light:

Guadeloupe Station

El Paso Natural Gas Company

There's no place to stay the night for at least 50 miles, and that is in Van Horn, the wrong direction, so I head for El Paso, over a hundred miles away Long magenta fingers paint across a rosy sky, already twinkling with evening stars. This long day will get longer before I sleep. So long, Number Two, thanks for the memories.

Near the beginning of my third year of school, my father was transferred again, this time to another gas company camp in Southeastern New Mexico— EPNG Company Station Number Three. Where did they get those creative names?

"Oh, you've been transferred to Number Three? Too bad, it's a hell hole."

The gas company employees just called it Number Three, located at Oil Center, not far from Jal, New Mexico, and it *was* a hell hole: "Number Three? Yeah, I spent a month there one week."

The most vivid memory of the time we lived there is that it never got dark. Employee housing was similar to Number Two, but the gas camp was larger, houses located closer to the gas operations, huge flare gas standpipes all around, roaring flames a hundred feet in the air, the sound of a wounded animal who never sleeps. The rumble of the flames and smell of burning flare gas permeated everything.

My mother hated it, and so did I. There was no place to play. At Number Two we had the vast, endlessly interesting desert and its wildlife. Here, we were just stuck out in the middle of nowhere in a flat, barren spot with no place to roam. School was more like the crowded one in El Paso, not the two-room school where I knew everyone. We had to line up to go everywhere: the playground, recess, the cafeteria, to catch the bus after school. To top it off, sitting right behind me, in the last desk in my row, was a boy who was sixteen years old. Can you believe it? Sixteen years old and in the third grade—what we used to do to handicapped children! Fortunately for me, he was a gentle giant who became my friend, probably because I treated him as one; no one else would have much to do with him.

18.

A sad event took us away from this place, and I was glad to go. In early 1945, we learned that my grandfather Caleb was gravely ill, and had moved to a small ranch west of Ft. Worth where he and my grandmother now lived with my uncle Hubert Reding, who was managing it for a wealthy absentee owner. My grandfather, at age 61, died in April of cancer. My father was hired to take over as foreman of the ranch, the Walker Place. We were going back to the country I loved, a void now in our lives. It would be many years before I realized the impact Caleb Reding had on my life.

For over 40 years my grandmother, Virginia Meyers Reding, had been a farm wife and mother, managing her home, raising five children, doing a man's work in the fields picking cotton, corn, whatever grew on the place, taking care of Caleb, doing whatever was necessary to keep hearth and home together. She had not had an easy life, and now at age 59 was alone, without a dime to her name or a place she could call home. For much of her married life, from the time she was fifteen, Jennie had struggled to make ends meet, to manage the family's meager resources during the downward spiral fraught by the Depression begun fifteen years earlier, but in reality for a much longer time—her family, and many others besides, had never known prosperous times.

With few other choices, too proud to live with any of her children, Jennie moved to Denton to live with an older sister, Clara Story, who had a large, rambling home on Sycamore Street, three blocks south of the Denton Square, where she took in boarders. Mama moved into a tiny cottage on Aunt Clara's property, a place with electricity but no indoor toilet, not much bigger than a chicken coop. She got a job as a dishwasher at a popular local eatery on Hickory Street a block east of the Square, making 35 cents an hour. In later years, as a high schooler, I worked as a dishwasher in that same café for a couple of weeks before I landed another, easier summer job doing farm work. Being a dishwasher was one of the toughest jobs I ever had!

Sound pretty bleak? It does as I read it now, but back then as kids when we went to Denton to visit Mama, it didn't seem bleak at all. But what do kids know of the hardships and struggles endured by their older family members?

Jerry and I always looked forward to these regular visits, when we ate Mama's homemade peanut butter cookies, the best ever, and on most of those Saturday afternoons walked up to the Square to see a double-feature movie, always a western, at one of the theaters on the west side of the Square—either the Dreamland, New Isis or Palace. Mama would give us a quarter, and with another quarter from Mom we could see a double feature western, with serials attached, for nine cents each, and have enough left over for a bag of popcorn or a candy bar. *Man, that was livin'!*

Mama's sister, Aunt Clara, had not had an easy life either, but instead had one filled with much hardship and quite a bit of notoriety, none of it her doing. Clara's husband was Nathan Story, who people said never did an honest day's work in his life. He was a small-time thief, a crook who tried to go big time by forming a gang patterned, I guess, after the

Clyde Barrow Gang. But the Story Gang was not as successful or notorious as Bonnie and Clyde, failing to successfully rob the banks at Justin or Krum as Bonnie and Clyde had done—yes, that same Krum Bank that had lost Papa's prize hunting horn.

By the time my grandmother moved to Denton, Nathan Story was serving a life sentence in Huntsville for murdering his girlfriend's other boyfriend. Truth wins out over fiction every time, except when movies are made. Tales of the Story Gang had morphed into a minor local legend by the time we moved to Denton in 1948, but were nothing compared to the stories told about some earlier notorious outlaws: Sam Bass, Belle Star and the famously swift Denton Mare, about whom a western movie was made starring Howard Duff and Ida Lupino.

19.

About a year ago, traveling west on Interstate 40 in Eastern New Mexico, passing an eighteen-wheeler, I noticed the logo on the side of the trailer:

B.F. Walker Trucking Company

Seeing that logo brought back a flood of memories. B.F. Walker had started a trucking company in Ft. Worth in the years before World War II, hauling defense contractor parts and equipment from the defense plants in Ft. Worth to El Paso and points west. Prospering, he bought a ranch west of Ft. Worth in Tarrant County, and another one near Santa Rosa, New Mexico. It was to the Tarrant County ranch we moved in the spring of 1945.

The Walker place was called a stock farm, a new term for me. It was a hobby farm, the owner lived in Ft. Worth, coming out to oversee the operation only on rare occasions; I remember seeing him only once. The farm/ranch raised beef cattle, registered Herefords, which my dad was expected to train, groom and show at fairs and stock shows. We also farmed enough land to grow feed for the cattle—oats, barley and hay. I got to help, and learned a lot about the art and science of breeding and showing cattle.

It was a side of my father I did not know. From the time he was sixteen until he married my mom, he had done farm and ranch work where his primary responsibility was caring for beef cattle that were raised for breeding and show stock. He knew a lot about show cattle.

It was here that I was finally able to live out many of my cowboy fantasies. There were horses to ride, calves to rope, landscape to explore, a big red barn that was perfect for western adventures, and to top it all off, Buster was there. I was in *hog heaven* again. I learned to drive the tall, green John Deere tractor, the "Poppin' Johnny", and had my first driving lessons in the International pickup.

Many of my adventures on the Walker place involved horses, both large and small. I had some hard lessons in the art of breaking horses. Well, little horses——Shetland ponies—and I came to believe that no ornerier critter ever existed, at least the ones I tried to gentle and train. A neighbor to the west of us raised Shetland ponies and pony/horse hybrids to train and sell to families with children. I was enlisted to help him break his ponies to lead and ride. But the truth is, they "broke" me more often than I broke them. Getting them to lead was not much of a problem, and getting them "saddle broke" was not so hard either, but the gentling part, the fine tuning, turning them into animals that were easy for children, was not easy at all.   I was kicked, bit, stepped on, thrown off and generally bullied by a number of ponies not much larger than Saint Bernards. I came away from that experience vowing never to own a Shetland pony, or a pony of any sort—they seemed to me to have developed a mean disposition just because they were smaller, determined to show the rest of the world they could be just as tough as the big guys, kinda like little guys needing to prove they were tough, like Jimmy Cagney in the movies. Get kids a regular horse, one trained to be gentle and easy with children. Our friend Bellamie's horses here in New Mexico are a good example.

There were all kinds of horses on the Walker place. The best of the lot was Buck, a tall (seventeen hands) grey cowhorse, about fifteen years old who was gentle and wise. But he was too big for me, so I chose Bomber, a beautiful half-Shetland, black, iron-mouthed and ornery. He was short enough to saddle easily, and was good for nothing much besides being my reluctant steed in the cowboy adventures I played out.

One of my favorites was to race Bomber through the large door of the big, L-shaped barn, grab an overhead rafter and swing off his back, hanging in mid-air before dropping down on unsuspecting, imaginary villains that were hot on my heels, the way I had seen the Durango Kid do it in the movies. Bomber would continue running, make a sharp left and continue on down the top of the "L" to the end of the barn. I had this move down pretty good, having practiced it a number of times, until one day I tried it and failed to get one of my boots out of a stirrup. Just as I grabbed the overhead rafter, I was jerked back and pulled off the saddle, falling to the ground, one leg caught in the stirrup.

Bomber continued running with me being drug on my back down the top of the "L" for about a hundred feet, to the end of the long hallway of the barn. Fortunately, the broad center hallway, with stalls for cattle and horses on either side, was fairly soft and covered with hay. The most embarrassing part was having my dad see me being drug, flat on my back, to the end of the runway, and him having to help me get my foot out of the stirrup. It probably hurt, but the humiliation was worse—the Durango Kid would never flub an overhead dismount like that!

Soon after we won Hitler's War, the servicemen began to come home, and there were a couple of marriages in our family. Two of Dad's sisters, Lavada and Roberta, got married, and Lavada and her new husband, Bill Griggs, stopped by for a visit during their honeymoon. The Gage side of my family has always been close, getting together for most of the Holidays—Thanksgiving, Christmas, Easter, Fourth of July. I was delighted to make the acquaintance of my new Uncle Bill, and to take them on a tour of the Walker place.

The next day after they arrived, we saddled up several horses and rode around, ending up on the back side of the ranch, a mile or so from the house. As we turned to head back, we noticed smoke and flames in the distance we had just covered—it was the beginning of a grass fire. Bill had tossed a burning cigarette down, catching the knee-high native grass on fire. It wasn't big yet, but the wind was fanning the flames and it was spreading. In a panic, we ran the horses back near where the fire began, quickly unsaddled, took the saddle blankets off and began beating the fire out with them. Working furiously, we were able to keep it from spreading. When it began to get away from us, we needed something else to help beat out the fire. Without a moment's hesitation, Bill yanked off his khakis and began fighting the fire with them, his white underwear and long, pale legs in stark contrast to the blackened grassland.

After some furious firefighting we managed to contain the blaze, my father having seen what was happening and drove the pickup over to us, water sloshing out of buckets hurriedly filled at the water trough. Using feed sacks soaked in water we finally snuffed it out. As we trudged back to the house over the acre or so of blackened prairie, relieved that the fire had been contained, we all had a good laugh at Bill's expense, his now soot-stained legs and darkened shorts a comical sight. Remembering this event, we have all had some chuckles over the years.

The Walker place provided us with most of what we needed. There was a large garden where we grew the vegetables we ate, a milk cow provided more milk than we needed, and once a week we went to Ft. Worth to sell the cream that we separated from the milk, and also the excess eggs our laying hens provided. This weekly excursion to Cowtown was a treat, one I looked forward to. One trip was an unforgettable experience.

There was a pattern to our journeys to town. We would first go to the South Ft. Worth location of Swift & Co. to sell the cream and eggs, and would then often go into downtown to Leonard Brothers, an all-purpose dry goods establishment that had a farm and ranch store where we purchased ranch supplies. We would then head back toward home, traveling down Camp Bowie Boulevard to Five Points, an area in West Ft. Worth where we would occasionally stop at a Texaco filling station to get soda pop.

On this one occasion, we had stopped at the gas station and were inside getting our case of sodas, when we heard a horrendous crash out front.

Knowing this must be a car crash, we rushed out to the street, witnesses to a terrible sight. A car full of black men had crashed headlong into a Coca Cola delivery truck.   There were broken Coke bottles everywhere, and at least two men in the crumpled car appeared to have been killed, and two others seriously injured lying, amid the broken glass on the street. Blood was everywhere.

One of the men in the street was crumpled on his side, groaning but not moving. The other man was lying on his back, also moaning and trying to get up. As he attempted to raise himself up, his scalp fell back from his head; he had literally been scalped! To this day, this memory is the most horrific of my life. For years afterward, there were recurring nightmares about this terrible accident.

My memory of this day is not just about this appalling event, it is also about the reaction of the white men who witnessed it. My father, Jerry and I were standing there, frozen in horror at the scene before us, when I heard one man say, "Them niggers were drunk, they got what they deserved."

Another said, "Niggers have tough hides, it won't hurt 'em much."

There was a powerful whisky smell mingled with the sweet Coca Cola and coppery odors of blood. To this day, the smell of bourbon triggers my gag reflex—I cannot drink it, can't stand it.

Up to that point, my life had been pretty sheltered, having spent most of my few years in the country, with limited contact with the rest of the world. I did not understand what these men were talking about, but I recognized the cold, cruel tone in their voices. Trying to understand, I turned to my dad to ask what they meant. My question died in my throat as I saw the look on his face. He had turned away from the crash scene, unable to look anymore. Horror and compassion mingled on his face, tears streamed down his cheeks. After helping the crash victims as much as we could, we left for home as the ambulance arrived.

The ride home was a silent one. My brother Jerry, four at the time, was also traumatized. Since my mother now worked at Montgomery-Wards in Ft. Worth, he was my father's constant companion, going everywhere with him, usually riding standing next to Dad holding on to his shoulder for balance, decades before seatbelts and child safety restraint laws. Jerry sat wide-eyed, huddled between us, and leaning his head on Dad's knee, finally went to sleep.

Later that evening Dad told Mom about the accident as supper was being prepared. Still shocked by the gory scene, I asked: "Why did those men talk that way?"

My mom looked at my dad, expecting him to speak. The crash had shaken him, too, and without speaking, turned and walked into the living room. There was a long silence. Finally, my mother answered, "There's a lot of mean folks in the world, Jimmy."

Up until this incident, I had been either too young, too sheltered or both, to know about racial prejudice. The rural Texas of my childhood was as much south as west. I had heard the word *nigger* a few times but paid little attention to it. I did not yet understand the bigotry behind the word. Most of my life had been spent with very little contact with people of color. When I began first grade in that crowded war-time El Paso elementary school, all schools in Texas and throughout the south were segregated, something else I did not yet understand.

In West Texas, where there were few, if any, African Americans, the segregation in schools extended to Mexican Americans. I saw brown-skinned children on the ranches or when we went to El Paso, but again, as a child it did not arouse any conscious wonderment. No one in my family ever talked about people of color, at least not in my presence. Schools were still segregated when I graduated from Denton High School in 1954. On the few occasions I saw Mexican American or African American children it never occurred to me that they went to *segregated* schools; I just thought they went to *different* schools.

The good news is that children are born color-blind. The bad news is that we begin to learn bigotry from adults at an early age. I thank God for my parents, who never disparaged people of color during my growing up years. As I got older and began to pay more attention to those things, I heard the "N" word used by relatives at family gatherings. In that regard, the Gage and Reding clans were probably no different than most southerners, but my parents were silent during those times, and rarely participated in such conversations.

Nona and JG were both people of their time, having grown up in an unforgiving, rural Texas environment where meager financial resources and fundamentalist religious beliefs were the order of the day. Yet each, by the unconditional love and constant support shown to Jerry and me, set an example of tolerance and acceptance so subtle it would take me many years to fully appreciate.

Don't get me wrong—I'm not trying to glorify my parents. They were flawed like everybody else, but they were perfect to me. Most children idolize their parents, as they should. It is what makes learning by example the most powerful teaching model. It is only as we get older and begin to see more of the world, more of different kinds of people, that our moms and dads get shrunk down to normal size. We begin to adopt other ideals, other heroes. My mother and father are still my heroes, always have been. I am blessed to have these two gentle souls as my parents.

Jim and Jerry Gage - circa 1944

One day a few weeks later, Jerry and I were playing in the hay loft of the barn, making a hideout by stacking bales into walls and a covering. We decided to play Lone Ranger and Tonto. Jerry, of course, was my faithful companion Tonto, and I tied him up to a rafter in the loft so that I could come back to rescue him from the villains who had captured him. I left him tied up the loft, went to the house for something, and forgot all about him. A couple of hours later, when mom came home from work, she asked, "Where's Jerry?" Uuh ohh! I slipped out of the house and raced to the barn loft and found Jerry still tied up, asleep, exhausted from yelling for me to come and untie him. I don't remember him agreeing to be Tonto after that.

My working life as a cowboy was sorely tested while we lived on the Walker place. Flights of fancy continued as I played out roles as Tom Mix, Gene Autry, and the Durango Kid. But reality was a harsh master. I was old enough now, at age nine, to help with chores and with the dozens of tasks that need doing around cattle and horses. There seems always to be more things that need doing than there is daylight in which to do them. Helping my dad grind feed was dusty work, lugging pails of cow cake and horse feed was heavy, hard work, and there was always a cow, calf or horse that needed some kind of doctorin'. Farm and ranch work is a 7/365 day occupation. I don't remember my folks ever taking a vacation.

The job I disliked the most, however, was feeding the hogs. We fed the excess milk from our milk cow to the hogs, and often as I poured the milk over the fence into their feed trough, an old sow who had a large litter of baby pigs would try to bite me as I leaned over the fence. She was mean, or maybe just protective of her little ones like all mamas are. Anyhow, we didn't dare climb into the hog pen with her.

One day as we were feeding the hogs, Jerry and I standing on a rung of the board fence, a gust of wind caught Jerry's straw hat and blew it into the hog pen. Quick as a wink, that old mama sow grabbed it in her mouth and chomped it down before we could try to retrieve it.   Jerry was distraught; he wore that straw hat everywhere.

Buster did not play as prominent a role in my life on the Walker place as he had when I was younger. He didn't seem to mind that our years apart, and our trek to West Texas and Eastern New Mexico had changed me. I was more interested in other things now: fantasy play, horses and heroes. I escaped each day into my favorite radio dramas, saved money to order a Tom Mix secret decoder ring, a Jack Armstrong pedometer and a Captain Midnight ring that glowed in the dark.

When I wasn't available, Jerry became Buster's companion; they went on forays to the nearby creek to look for crawdads, tadpoles and other critters. And each day, Buster went on his own hunting trips, sometimes returning with his canine smile, other times coming back tired and streaked with mud. Once he returned late, limping, with a nasty gash on his shoulder, probably the result of a fight with a larger animal, tame or wild I couldn't say. He wouldn't allow Mom to tend to his wound, and laid up under the house for several days, only coming out to eat table scraps.

Our house was a conventional Texas ranch house, with a large front porch and a pier-and-beam foundation elevated about eighteen inches off the ground. One day, soon after we had moved there, Buster chased a skunk under the house and killed it under my bedroom floor. The skunk smell was awful. Jerry and I had to sleep on the living room couch for several weeks, until the skunk scent lessened. Every time it rained, the skunk smell came back, and that winter, during a particularly long rainy spell, we slept in the living room for about a month.

We lived on the Walker place less than two years—it seems longer now—there are so many memories: Riding along with neighboring ranchers on day-long cattle drives; helping Dad show cattle at the Ft. Worth Stock Show; riding Bomber the two miles to my two-room Chapin School, where suspicions that Santa Claus wasn't real were confirmed when I recognized my dad's cowboy boots on Santa's feet. I think most of us still cling to a fragment of this Christmastime childhood belief—how else to explain this magical time of year?

20.

In the fall of 1946, a few weeks after school started, we moved again. Dad had taken a job as manager of Cherry Hills Stock Farm, near Louisville, Kentucky. The farm was beautiful, with dark green pastures edged all around by white fences, and a large, white two-story barn built into the side of a hill so that you could drive the pickup or tractor into the second story loft. The farm was pastoral, picture-postcard pretty, like an English countryside. Cherry Hills Stock Farm raised registered polled Herefords; the owner was a wealthy Louisville businessman. This was the first move I remember not wanting to make; I loved living on the Walker place, close to Gage and Reding family members.

Since we moved after school had started, I began fifth-grade there as a stranger, and made few friends. Jerry was in first grade now, and we kept pretty much to ourselves. I felt like an outsider, like I didn't belong. Another thing I remember about that year in school was everyone had to line up in the cafeteria to take a series of vaccinations, the nurse jabbing a needle into my arm, hurting so much I wanted to cry. To this day I detest having to get a shot or having a needle stuck in me for any reason, sometimes to the point of passing out.

Not long after we moved to Kentucky, just before Halloween, our friends the Davises arrived for a visit. The two boys, Ray and Jimmy, had been runnin' buddies when we lived at Number 2 in West Texas; it was a real treat to have someone we knew to pal around with up there in that north country. We had fun making a hay bale fort in the barn loft, having rubber gun fights, going for hikes in a nearby wooded area so rough, dense and foreign it seemed right out of the Lost World. The wooded area was rugged and wild, with lots of trees, bushes, rock overhangs, shallow caves and streams everywhere—very different from the familiar rolling prairie of Texas.

One day we ventured deep into the wooded area, farther than I had ever been. As we played on the bank of a clear, shallow creek, watching the small fish, minnows and water striders, I looked up to see a large animal glaring crazily down at us. Across a distance of about 50 yards, higher up on a rocky ledge overlooking the creek, a huge dog, shaggy like a St. Bernard, glared down on us through his one good eye. He was foaming at the mouth, his other eye dangled down his face, hanging by a thread of tissue. When I pointed him out to the Davis boys, they looked up the canine apparition for a few moments, then Ray began to run away, yelling, "Rabies, he's got rabies!" Jimmy hurried after him.

I didn't know what rabies looked like, but if Ray said it was rabies, he was older and must know, so I tore off after them, looking back over my shoulder often to see if the dog was chasing us. We didn't stop running until we got out of the woods, and continued hurrying to the house where we excitedly reported sighting the mad dog to our parents. Later, my dad and Mr. Davis went down to the spot where we had seen the rabid dog, but he was gone.

The next day being Halloween, we decided to skip the treats, and go right to the tricks, as ornery little boys will sometimes do. Across the road from the farm lived a very nice retired couple, the Williams, with whom our family had made friends. Mrs. Williams would give us cookies fresh from the oven, and Mr. Williams sometimes took us to the store in his "machine". In spite of their kindnesses, and because of their proximity, we decided to "trick" them, with a little encouragement from the Davis' boys.

Late in the afternoon, about sundown, we placed a note under a rock on their front porch, knocked on the door, then scurried across the road and hid in the bar ditch. When Mrs. Williams answered the door, she knocked the rock off the note, saw it, reached down, picked it up and read it: "YOU WILL DIE AT MIDNIGHT!"

When the prank was conceived, we thought it was hilarious, but soon changed our tune. Mrs. Williams showed the note to her husband, they went back inside the house, and a few minutes later she came across the road and knocked on our front door. My mom answered the door, and they went inside together. Uh Ooh. This looks serious. We continued to hide in the ditch, now afraid of what might happen.

A few minutes later, my mom came to the front door and yelled, "Jimmy Allen, you boys come here!"

The jig was up. Any time my mom called me Jimmy Allen, I knew I was in trouble. We later learned that the Williams' were frightened when they read the note, wondered about calling the sheriff, and came over to our house to consult with our parents about what to do. Needless to say, we were in big trouble. The hardest part of the punishment was having to go over to the Williams' house, confess to our crime, and apologize. Fortunately, all was forgiven. Knobby-kneed boys can be stinkers, can't they?

When school was out in May 1947, we made what had become almost an annual move, back to Texas this time for a brief summer stint on the 3-D Ranch near Arlington, and then on to the Northwoods Stock Farm, north of Ft. Worth. Here Dad would be a herdsman for the show cattle, registered polled Herefords. The owner, Mr. Watts, was publisher of the *Ft. Worth Star Telegram.* I would be a sixth-grader at Saginaw Elementary School.

Rememberances? A few, such as helping Dad groom and train the show cattle; my first girl friend, Sheila Lockhart, whose birthday was on February 29, leap year (and therefore only 3 years old!) being involved in 4-H, judging milk cows (I was terrible), and listening weekly to the Light Crust Doughboys from Burris Mills, a large flour mill in Saginaw where Jerry and I went to school.

Why the Light Crust Doughboys? Because Bob Wills and his band *were* the Light Crust Doughboys, and I have loved Bob Wills' country swing music all my life. W. Lee "Pappy" O'Daniels was then a candidate for Governor of Texas, and the Light Crust Doughboys traveled around with him as he campaigned across the state from the flatbed of a truck, with Bob Wills playing and singing everywhere he went. O'Daniels was the owner of Burris Mills, and "Pass the Biscuits, Pappy" was a popular moniker he was tagged with.

In February, Northwoods Stock Farm showed their cattle at the Southwestern Exposition and Stock Show in Ft. Worth, one of the largest stock shows in the country. It is a huge operation, and I got to stay overnight in the dorm which housed the men and boys who were showing cattle. The stock show also has a rodeo, billed as the largest indoor rodeo in the world. The special guest that year was the "Singing Cowboy" Gene Autry and his Wonder Horse, Champion. Seeing one of my cowboy movie heroes in person was a once-in-a-lifetime thrill.

In the summer of 1948, we left the farm for the last time and moved to Denton, which has been my parent's home for over 50 years. My vagabond childhood was over. Concerned that our itinerant farm life would not allow Jerry and me to be in a place where we could get a good education, Mom and Dad moved us to this familiar North Texas college town. Looking back on those years in Denton, I don't think you could find a better place to grow up—my high school and college years were filled with good times, good friends and lively, interesting experiences. But then, so were the first twelve years of my life!

21.

<u>The Denton Years</u>

The move to Denton in 1948 marked a major change in our lives. Without saying so, my parents had decided to stay in one place, put down roots, and join a community. Mom and Dad never mentioned this, but I'm also sure that they were tired of the constant moves they had made over the years.

Denton was a good choice, familiar from our years of living within a 30 mile radius, but nevertheless it extracted a high price from my parents, particularly my father who missed farm and ranch life, the only life he really had ever known. He immediately got a job at Moore Business Forms, Inc., the largest private employer in the county. Dad went to work in the Stock Department, which handled all the paper on which the jillions of business forms were printed, primarily for federal government consumption, the feds being Moore's largest contractor. He was to work in the stock department at various jobs both

~ 176 ~

monotonous and demanding for the next 25 years, retiring as foreman on the day he turned 62.

My mother worked at various jobs, first at North Texas as a cook in Chilton Hall, the dorm where the college athletes lived and ate, and later at a succession of jobs where her seamstress skills were used throughout most of the remainder of her working life. Mom was a superb seamstress, a professional, who made virtually all her own clothing throughout her life, clothes for her sons, grandchildren (with a particular liking for granddaughters' clothing—both Dana and Jenny had a closet full of "Nona Originals" fancy girls' duds).

During her high school years Mom had dreamed of going to college, but she was both victim and a product of the times. Few women from Wise County, Texas went to college, fewer still who grew up with the scant resources available to her. Beneath her quiet and shy demeanor lurked a keen intelligence—she had the ability to be almost anything, and throughout her life utilized this intelligence and her creativity to coble together a lovely home environment for her family on a meager budget. Her dream of going to college, which would have been easy in this town where there were two of them, was to be realized vicariously through her two sons, both graduates of North Texas.

As a gawky kid on the edge of adolescence, I knew little of this at the time. In later years, when a looking-back compulsion tugged me in that direction, the people who were my parents take on more complete personas with wants and needs that have little to do with me. A long, slow extraction process over several of these later years uncovered buried nuggets of thwarted desires secretly held.

Both Nona and JG were reticent, shy, of-their-times, unable or unwilling to share feelings or dreams, muzzled by a lifetime of limited resources and unrealized dreams such as owning their own farm, or Mom going to college. On one teary day, Mom, now 91 and wheelchair-bound at Good Samaritan Nursing Home, sad and lonely and feeling helpless, poured out her pent-up dreams, held for three-quarters of a century, in a rush of heartbreaking candor. They were dreams I knew nothing about: dreams of an intelligent, vibrant and stunning young woman yearning to escape the hard-scrabble existence of her growing-up years, but accepting, as we all must do to retain our sanity, the harsh realities of day-to-day living.

It has only been through decades of living, working, trying to raise my own children, making mistakes, that I have come to realize what huge sacrifices my parents made for Jerry and me. No child can ever repay this priceless gift to a mom or dad, but maybe a down-payment can be made by trying to be there for my children and grandchildren.

1948 – 1954

There's probably no one but me interested in these six years of my junior high and high school years, so I'll hit a few high spots, and talk some about these times.   As mentioned before, Denton was an ideal town (population 25,000) in which to grow up. Our first home was on Norman Street, a modest two-bedroom about a mile south of the
Downtown Square and from my schools.

In junior high we walked everywhere—to school, to the movies, on dates, to athletic practices and games—at least until we were old enough to drive and could talk our parents out of the family car for a date night on Fridays or Saturdays. No one went out on week nights during the school year, and usually not much during the summer months either, unless you were going to a softball game in the park or perhaps a brief visit with a girlfriend or pal.

Even in high school, almost no one had a car. I can remember the DHS parking lot having only the teacher's cars, and maybe a few others. A couple of friends, Spencer Miller because he had a substantial paper route, and Terrell King, whose family ranched and had several oil wells, had cars. Terrell, a life-long friend, got a new 1952 Ford during his junior year, and would sometimes give me a ride to school. We also double-dated on a number of occasions, him driving of course. For high school graduation, I got a 1941 Chevrolet Club Coupe, a great car I drove throughout my college days. My dad's cousin, Victor Ray Gage, bought the Chevy from me and drove it as a work car for the next ten years.

Entertainment? There was no TV until the early 50s, but there were Friday night ballgames and Saturday night movies at the Campus Theater, or a Stage Show at the NT Auditorium. In junior high the

Stage Show was almost an every Saturday night event. For ten cents—yeah, that's a *dime*—you got live musical and comedy performers, most very good, and 'Fessor Graham and his Aces playing popular and jazz numbers—they were great! You also got a movie short or serial and a movie, a rerun, but very few I had seen. What a bargain, even for 1950.

The decade of the 50s was a special time for me, as I'm sure it was for most of my friends and classmates as we grew from early adolescence to young adulthood. It was a time of tremendous growth, opportunity and change, when nothing seemed out of reach or impossible to achieve. Have we had a decade so full of promise since that time?

It was a great time and place to be an adolescent. We often traveled on foot with a few friends, guys or gals together, sometimes with dates, sometimes without—no such thing as gangs back in those days, at least not in Denton. The streets and parks were always safe, few parental concerns about where we were or where we went. Our parents knew where we were going and what time we were expected to be home. I don't remember ever getting a date home after her curfew. Wow, how the times have changed!

One of the great things about Denton was that it was and is a college town. Two colleges, actually—North Texas State College (now UNT) and Texas State College for Women (now TWU), for many years the only state-supported college for women in the U.S. We lived about a mile from the NT campus and I often walked across the campus on my way to or from nearby activities or friends' houses. When near the campus I always took the opportunity to walk through the Student Union Building. There were so many things going on there I wanted to see and know about—my favorite was going to the SUB around noontime to hear the twelve-O'clock or one-O'clock Lab Bands play, which they did on most days, almost always swing or jazz numbers.

At the time, and for many years afterward, NT was known to have one of the best Schools of Music, especially jazz, in the U.S.—rated in the Top Five, up there with Boston U., University of Michigan, Juliard—they were hot, and still are as far as I know. During the warm months, which was most of the time, it was a rarity to walk across campus without hearing vocal or instrumental music being practiced. Later, during the Vietnam War, the NT Lab Band was the only university band invited there to play for the troops. My love for jazz began during those cross-campus treks.

Academics were always fairly easy for me, at least I didn't have to study very hard, which was a good thing because in high school I majored in sports and minored in girls.

In sports I played football, basketball and ran track. Not a very good basketball player, I was better at football and probably best at track. In order to letter in track you had to place in the district track meet, which I did as a sophomore in the half-mile (880 yards), and was one of only three sophomores to letter. As a junior I eked out a place in the regional meet, and also ran a leg on the mile relay team, which also qualified for regional.

I was only a fair football player, but good enough to be a starter as an end my senior year (no flankers or wide-receivers in those days). A highlight for me was catching five passes, one for a TD, in the first half of the Paris game that year. That made up a little for the terrible skunking we endured in the Paris game the year before, when in the last game of the season in late November it was very cold and snowy, a frozen turf, we were beaten 53–0. Ouch! I mean, they beat the snot out of us, knocked three of our guys out of the game—Garland Warren, one of our best players (who later starred for the NT Eagles and played pro ball in Canada) was knocked out cold, woke up a few minutes later, ran back into the game and lined up on the Paris side of the ball and tackled our quarterback.

These guys were good, going all the way to the State Championship before losing by one point to Temple. They also had a winning tradition—their head coach was the father of Raymond Berry, now in the NFL Hall of Fame, one of the stars of the Baltimore Colts led by Johnny Unitas. Their major star this year was Gene Stallings, who later played on the famous Texas A&M National Championship team coached by Bear Bryant, played pro ball for a number of years and later followed Bear Bryant as coach at Alabama.

I was also the leading pass receiver my senior year, but that's not saying very much because we were primarily a running team. I always thought we had a lot of good athletes, particularly in football, but we only won five games our senior year (which was, however, the most games a DHS team won during my high school years). Several teammates went on to play college ball, and a couple made it to the pros. We had the fastest half-back in the District, Lee Amyx, who as a sprinter was almost never beaten and set the state broad jump record during our senior year. Our quarterback, Dub Land, tall and rangy, perhaps the best all-around athlete in school, also starred in basketball and was good enough in baseball to pitch AAA ball for five years before throwing his arm out. Dub was a good passer and I was his favorite receiver, since I could catch almost everything he threw my way.

In later years, at maybe our 25th or 30th high school reunion, several of us attending our D Club Luncheon (D Club being sport lettermen) were talking about our coaches and their coaching, or lack thereof. We all agreed the best coach during those years had been Eliott Smith, our junior high football coach. Mr. Smith, also a great math and shop teacher, really got in there and taught/showed us how to do all the fundamentals. He never yelled or cursed, and was a tough taskmaster. He brought out the best in us, and our ninth grade team was undefeated during an eight game season. We were feeling a little cocky after our team outscored the high school B Team during a scrimmage; we had high hopes as we went on to high school.

This D Club conversation was an eye-opener. For years I harbored the belief that we had been poorly coached in high school and did not know several of my teammates felt the same way. In both track and football I got very little individual attention, learned most of what I knew from observation, not from instruction. We agreed that our coaches were poor teachers; OK in other respects, but not as coaches.

Woulda', coulda', shoulda'. That water passed under the bridge a long time ago. As Marlon Brando said in a famous movie quote: "I coulda' been a contender," *I* coulda' been better, *we* could have been better, and on that Class of '54 reunion day, several of us agreed with a bit of bittersweet nostalgia. We all want to go out as winners.

I dated several girls in high school, none seriously until my junior year when someone I had secretly wanted to date finally broke up with her boyfriend. Today it seems in that more simple 50's boy/girl time relationships were more clearly defined and straightforward. You dated somebody, or more than one somebody, or you went "steady," which meant you agreed not to date someone else.

Well, maybe not always so clear, because with the storm of hormones constantly raging there was: going with someone, going steady, breaking up, going with someone else, then perhaps going steady with that person, or a new person. Doesn't sound so simple now, does it? Well, you just had to be there— the lines, if not always clear, were at least understandable to us at the time.

Jolene Embry, a year ahead of me, hung with a tight knit group of popular senior girls, who along with a few of the guys they went out with, were leaders in almost all areas of high school life. One of these girls was always getting elected to something: Homecoming Queen, Most Beautiful, Friendliest Girl. Jolene was elected Valentine Sweetheart that year. She had always smiled and been friendly toward me but we had never really said much other than "Hello." We were members of the same church—no small matter in those days, at least to our parents. Her father was an Elder at the Pearl St. Church of Christ; my dad was a Deacon at the Welch St. Church.

When I heard she had broken up with her boyfriend, I made my move. We started dating, clicked, and went steady for the rest of that school year and through the summer while she went to summer school at NT.

First love—Do you remember how it felt, how *you* felt, how the world looked? For me, it was like slowly waking up from a dream, seeing with a sharper vision, smells and sounds more distinct and vivid. I wanted to be at my best, be the best I could be, because at my best was the only acceptable way, so I got better, was better. At least that was the way it seemed to me, and if no one else noticed, that was O.K.

I got better in track and football, and during spring training, improved enough in football to be named as first team right end; the Denton paper quoted our coach as saying I was one of the most improved players on the team. My grades, always pretty good, got better. At the time, not knowing what this rush of emotions were, I couldn't have identified them, but they sure felt good, and now from my long-range view six decades later, it was *love.*

Throughout those years I almost always had a part-time job, and worked full-time at numerous jobs during the summers. Starting with a paper route in seventh grade, then was a soda jerk for two summers, washed cars and pumped gas at a Texaco Station, delivered flowers for Selby's Flower Shop, worked at Baird and Beck's Auto Repair Shop doing auto body grunt work, and more than anything else did farm work of all kinds—threshing oats, mowing and bailing hay, building fence, feeding and tending beef cattle, countless other chores done around a farm—work I knew how to do.

During the summer before my senior year I bit off more than I could chew. During the day I did farm work, mostly cutting and bailing hay for a prosperous, hard-working business man/farmer, Eddie Williams, who also owned the Eagle Motel in town, where I worked, after getting about four or five hours of sleep, as the night clerk from eleven p.m. to seven a.m. I wore myself out, lost weight, and had a hard time getting back in shape for my final year of high school football.

One last episode from that senior year summer: Three other friends and I were hanging out one evening, sitting in lawn chairs at the entrance to Schmitz Furniture Store, which fronted Schmitz Funeral Home, located on the narrow street one block north of the Denton Courthouse Square, the downtown center where many retail businesses were located. Two of my friends, Bob Jackson and Bill Tilley, along with Bob's older brother Brice, lived and worked at the funeral home at night driving the ambulance.

In those days there were no public ambulances; the only ones were owned by the three funeral homes in the area, taking turns responding to accident reports. They had radio systems tuned to the police and sheriff departments, listening for reported accidents with possible injuries. When an accident-related injury was reported, two of the guys would tear downstairs, hop in the ambulance, sirens and flashing lights on, and race out to the location of the accident.

On this evening, another funeral home ambulance service was up, so the guys were off for the night, sitting around, shooting the bull, and at some point we came up with an idea, started kicking it around, having some fun with it, when down the street walked three kids who were the solution to our idea. We looked at each other with a nod and a smile, and launched our plan.

Bob took the lead: "Hey, fellas, how y'all doin'?

"Good."

"Fine."

"OK."

After some reluctance we enticed them over for a chat, so we pulled out more metal lawn chairs for them to sit, and we were off to the races.

"How would you boys like to make a little money, say 50 cents?"

"Yeah, that'd be OK; whadda we have to do; we gotta git home pretty soon," each boy said in turn. They were lanky kids, about eleven or twelve years old, out for a night of summer fun.

"This won't take long, only about 30–45 minutes. We've been pretty busy this evening," Bob said smoothly. "Just got back from an ambulance call and want to get something to eat, but we need you guys to stay here while we go because someone has to watch over the body that just came in." As we began talking, Bill Tilley got up and quietly moved to the back of the store, becoming invisible in the darkness, no lights on in the store, shadows and darkness toward the rear.

As the word "body" was mentioned, two of the boys jumped up and started moving away, the third boy jerked up in his chair and looked at Bob, fear showing in his wide-eyed stare. Bob leaned over closer to the boy, saying "You're not scared, are you? We just picked this guy up and can't leave him alone until he's identified by someone. All we need you to do is keep an eye on him for a few minutes 'til we get back."

With that he got up and headed for the back, motioning the seated boy to follow him. "C'mon, I'll show you. He's covered up. You won't have to *see* him, just keep an eye on him." Bob kept moving toward the back of the store, coaxing the boy, and now all three boys, toward a closed door that led to the funeral area where the bodies were prepped for burial. The kids were very reluctant at first, but both Bob Chaney (our other friend with us this night) and I were also quietly encouraging the boys toward the prep room. They now moved back with us, along a long, wide, dark aisle crowded with all kinds of new and used furniture.

As Bob reached the funeral parlor door, he opened it and stood at the entrance, encouraging the boys to have a look. They did, very cautious at first, but when they saw a body covered by a large white sheet lying on a large metal gurney, each boy stood there and stared at the covered figure. "First time to see a dead body?" Bob asked. Each one nodded "yes."

One boy, the tallest, said, "I saw my granddad at his funeral in church. It was kinda creepy."

"Well, you won't hafta' look at this one, just keep an eye on things while we get something to eat, OK? We'll be back in a few minutes." With that the three of us began moving back up the aisle to the front of the store. As we began walking down the sidewalk in front, I looked back at the boys standing there in the open doorway, not going any closer.

We knew what was coming next, so we crept down the front of the store and waited in the near-darkness. In less than a minute one of the boys hurried up the furniture store aisle, running into a metal lawn chair, sending it clanging into a cluster of other lawn furniture. What a racket! A moment later a second boy sprinted down the same aisle, hurdling the jumble in front of him, and tore off down the street. The third boy, not far behind, ran into several overturned chairs, an ever louder clatter this time; he, too, tore off down the street passing the second boy like he was standing still—he was fast!

By now the two Bobs and I were laughing so hard we could hardly stand, and when Bill Tilley came through the funeral prep door still wearing the sheet and saying "Boo, Boo, Boo!!!" we had to sit down. We were laughing so hard we couldn't stand. The four of us, lifelong friends and later Sig Ep fraternity brothers, had many chuckles over this prank in later years.

PART 2. LATER

22.

Denton, 1954-57

It's the end of May and I am a high school graduate! My high school years have been great, but I am eager to begin a new phase of my life so start college classes at North Texas State here in Denton just ten days after graduation. Truth be told, my motivation to enter college life quickly is probably more toward the social than the academic.

My high school sweetheart, Jolene Embry, graduated a year ago and is also in summer school at UNT; we are in the early stages of rekindling a cooled-off romance. And my male ego has been stoked—I have met some college guys who are talking to me about pledging a fraternity, something I knew nothing about until a few weeks ago.

My mother now worked as the seamstress for the Boston Store, located on the Northeast corner of the Denton Square. Mom did all the alterations for the store, at that time one of the two largest dry goods stores in town, the other larger store was Russell's, on the Southwest corner of the Square. One day while visiting Mom at work I met Al Stockard, who worked part-time there while going to school at NT. Al was a Sig Ep, and as we visited back and forth a couple of times, he invited me to meet a couple of his fraternity brothers and invited me over to the fraternity house. I liked what I saw, and I guess they did too.

So, Wow! I'm feeling pretty big for my britches right now! By summer's end I am back down to normal size—Freshman English has a way of doing that, as does a soured romance.

My world had begun to expand, and would do so exponentially in the weeks and months ahead. But that's what growing up is all about, ain't it?

As I was going through high school graduation exercises, the U.S. Supreme Court was ruling on perhaps the most important case since the Civil War, <u>Brown vs. Board of Education</u>. This momentous ruling which desegregated the schools meant little to me at the time in my narrow world at DHS, but that soon changed.

North Texas was the first public college in Texas to integrate, beginning in 1955, and Texas being a southern as well as a western state might expect some racial unrest and even violence. We are all too familiar with the racial violence that erupted throughout the South during the 50s and 60s. That did not happen in our part of Texas, and I came to believe the reason it didn't at NT is grounded in the social and cultural fabric of the state—football.

Denton High School was a segregated school when I graduated. There was a black high school, Fred Moore, on the east side of town, and we did not mingle. The second time I was nudged into paying attention to the impact of segregation on my daily life was in 1952 when Dwight Eisenhower came to town to make a campaign speech that summer on the Denton Square. It was very hot and I was thirsty, so made my way through the crowd to get a drink in the basement of the Courthouse, perhaps for the first time. Stepping down into that grungy public spot I noticed two water fountains labeled "White" and "Colored."

This is not right, I thought, but kept my thoughts to myself. I don't recall much animosity, but separate races in our little Texas college town were taken for granted.

During my second year at NT in 1955, that all changed when an electrifying halfback from Ft. Worth showed up on the North Texas State Eagles football team that fall. Abner Haynes started as a freshman, the first black man to do so, and during the next four years his football heroics made us all color blind. He went on to All-American honors, later starring for the Dallas Texans, and when Lamar Hunt lost the storied coin flip to Clint Murcheson, owner of the Dallas Cowboys, they moved as part of the merger of the AFL and NFL, and became the Kansas City Chiefs. In Texas, football is King, and trumps everything else, even race. I don't recall any acts of racial violence in Texas until the assassination of Martin Luther King in 1968.

By the end of my first summer at NT I was eager to dive into college life and did so that September by being elected to the student senate and by pledging a fraternity, Sigma Phi Epsilon. I was riding high! I've always felt I lucked out by becoming a Sig Ep. What a great group of guys! We had numerous campus leaders: varsity athletes in football, basketball and track, class and student body presidents as well as the highest academic standing of any fraternity. We also had a lot of fun!

College fraternity and sorority life at North Texas in the 50's was scaled very differently than it became a few years later. Enrollment at NT in the fall of 1954 was 4,500 and growing. There were only eight national frats and two locals. There were six sororities, all housed in a college dorm quadrangle, Chilton Hall, now modified for the six sets of girls, the dorm which earlier housed the college athletes where my mom was a cook when we first moved to Denton. All girls had to be in their dorm by 10:50 on week nights and midnight on weekends. All students had to live in the dorm unless you were a local and lived at home (me), or were married. Sound like a different world? It was, but it did not seem nearly as restrictive then as it does now. It was a different time.

College social life was abuzz with a myriad of offerings—there was often a dance to go to, a performance or college event to attend—always with a major focus on fraternity/sorority life. Jolene and I had rekindled our romance. She pledged a sorority, Chi Omega, at the same time I was a Sig Ep pledge, and after we became members, were *pinned* at a midnight ceremony on the quadrangle at Chilton Hall. A pinning ceremony was the next thing to becoming engaged; a number of my fraternity brothers and her sorority sisters were pinned during our years at NT.

All this because I fell for a lovely young woman who was easy to be with, who shared many of my same values, whose parents liked me and I liked them, as mine did her. Jolene was an important part of my life for three years, with some starts and stops all budding romances seem to go through, more on than off, but the year she graduated, a year ahead of me, she went to work as a buyer at Sanger-Harris in Dallas, I looked away for a moment and she was gone, married an older guy she worked with.

I've always maintained that I got two educations as an undergraduate at North Texas: The first an academic one at which I was OK, managing to get a Liberal Arts degree in Government (Political Science) with a minor in History in three years by going to summer school two summers. The second and more significant one was a social education, at which I was pretty good. I learned a lot about myself and people and how to deal with them, becoming very active in all aspects of fraternity and college life. Maturing into young adulthood I began to gain a self-confidence not present before as I realized I was good with people and was developing some leadership skills.

During my undergraduate years I always had at least one part-time job, sometimes two or more: I continued to do some farm work and occasionally delivered flowers for Selby's Flower Shop, worked for Emmett Brown at the Singer Sewing Center cleaning and servicing sewing machines, and making daily house calls throughout Denton County. Emmett's father had been our rural delivery mailman when we lived in Wise County during my childhood. Our two families had some long-term connections.

My dog Buster was a selective car chaser, singling out the old Chevy mail car on our rural road with little traffic. For some reason he didn't like Mr. Brown's car, perhaps because it always stopped while mail was put in the mailbox. He would try to bite one of the tires as it stopped. One day he bit at a front tire and was run over by the front wheel. I was horrified when I saw it happen and ran out to see how he was. Mr. Brown stopped and got out—he was also upset. Buster lay on the ground for a few moments—I thought he was dead—then got up, hobbled off, going under the house whimpering what I feared were his final sounds. Fortunately the mail car was an older lightweight Chevy which did not crush him like one of today's heavyweights would do. He lay under the house for a couple of days, finally coming out to eat something, limping and gaunt. I never saw him chase another car.

23.

During the long Texas drought of the 1950's a joke---probably already as old as the state---was told again and again about a man who bet several of his friends that it would never rain again, and collected from two of them.

Elmer Kelton, *The Time It Never Rained*

This drought was one of the longest on record, lasting seven years, finally ending in the spring of my last undergraduate year at North Texas. But in truth, dry spells have been part of the climate conditions in the area of Texas where I grew up for decades, perhaps centuries. Kelton also says: "Each new generation tends to forget—until it confronts the sobering reality—that dryness has always been the normal condition in the western half of the state. Wet years have been the exceptions."

Both sets of my grandparents struggled to eke out a living on their Wise County farms during dry spells of the '20s and '30s. An earlier drought that began in 1941 may have been the final climatic blow.

Both Caleb and Merlin, strong-willed and individualistic, were forced by the bruising demands of that uncompromising land and resulting health issues to retreat for a brief time before death overtook them.

Some western authors and climatologists agree on how the land changes west of the 98th meridian, which bisects Wise and Denton counties. A road sign on I-20 at the city limits reads: "Fort Worth, Where the West Begins."

A drought by Texas standards does not necessarily mean no rainfall; rains may fall, occasionally, but they are usually light and moisture from one rainfall seldom remains until the next.

What I remember about those years is that it rarely rained during the time I did farm work, or the two summers I worked with my good friend Al Stockard on his father's City of Dallas Water Department crew, which was charged with keeping obstructions and log jams out of the creek that was a major source of water from Lake Dallas to the city's water pumping stations. Hot and dry is how I remember those summers. And then the weather changed.

On a day in the middle of May I drove to Dallas to visit a girl I was dating at the time. I remember the day as hot and muggy with high humidity, intermittent rain, storm clouds all around. After my visit, heading home north on the Stemmons Freeway I happened to look in my rearview mirror: It was a scary sight. A huge dark cloud centered over the Oak Cliff section of Dallas seemed to be coming in my direction; this large blue/black/green cloud, funnel-shaped and ominous, was hurling large pieces of debris high up in the sky. I drove away from the storm cloud as fast as I could through very heavy rain and wind. It was tense ride home, rain pounding so hard I had to slow down to let the windshield wipers catch up with the downpour.

We learned later that afternoon that the Oak Cliff tornado had done extensive damage and killed several people. There was more to come.

The storm had abated somewhat as I drove into Denton; heavy, threatening clouds were massing west of town, forming what looked like another tornado funnel out around Krum, about ten miles away. Pulling into our driveway on Alice Street, I sloshed into the house, the water in our yard ankle-deep. Mom and Dad, already home from work, were looking out the back door.

"Jimmy, did you see that?" Mom asked, pointing toward the west. The western property line of our yard ended at a small creek which meandered through this part of town before it flowed into the larger Denton Creek a mile or two away. Today this creek was a torrent swollen beyond its usual bounds and now already fifty yards wide, covering most of our back yard. Mom was not talking about the flooding creek, but about the tornado funnels now moving in the distance. Yes, I said *funnels*, because there were not just two, but three funnel clouds scattered across the western horizon; the one to the north was over near Krum, the one to the south seemed about where Justin was, the one in the middle seemed to be a bit smaller but was closer to us and pretty scary.

How many people have even seen a tornado funnel cloud, much less two, would you believe *three* at one time? Well, if you live or have traveled through Tornado Alley, maybe so. For two- or three-hundred miles east or west of us, and perhaps a thousand miles north or south, we were confronted each spring and early summer with weather conditions conducive to tornadoes.

This time we were fortunate: The northern-most tornado touched down near Krum, doing some damage, but leaving no casualties; the one to the south was on the ground for a brief time near Justin but did little damage. The one in the middle moved around for a while but did no damage because it was centered in a rural area where few people lived.

The flooded creek continued to rise, the rain continued to fall. As some wag might say: "Man, that was a frog-strangler, a turd-floater; it rained like a cow peeing on a flat rock off a forty foot bluff!" And so it was, water rising until all of Alice Street was flooded along several blocks down to where the street ended into Congress Avenue and Denton High School, water rising up until it was just an inch from coming into our front door. And come in it did later that afternoon when a fire truck moving slowly down our street created a wave just high enough to wash into our front door, getting the carpet in the living room soaked with rainwater.

24.

Graduating from college in May, 1957 with a Liberal Arts degree qualified me for almost nothing except going on to graduate school. I did have a direction, however, and headed to the big city, Dallas, to find a job and enroll at SMU Law School. I could not afford to go to law school full-time; had to have a job, so began interviewing with insurance companies and practically any one else in Dallas that the NT Placement Office said had openings. After several interviews I had to admit that except for a sparkling personality I had little to offer the business world. Being a BMOC and a leader in my fraternity extended no further than the edge of the college campus—no businesses in Dallas were hiring Charm School graduates!

Discouraged and wondering what I was going to do to make a living, my savior came in the form of my aunt, Lavada Griggs, who was a third-grade teacher in Irving, a few miles west of Dallas. The superintendent of schools was a friend of hers, she talked to him about me, called me up in mid-June and asked, "Jimmy, have you ever thought about teaching school? There are a couple of openings at Crockett Junior High School, and I'm pretty sure you can get one."

The truth was I hadn't thought much about teaching, but I sure would think about it now if a job was in the offing! I was not having much luck job-hunting and was a step away from taking a job with the FBI for slave-labor wages, a job I didn't particularly want, but it would allow me to go to night law school.

But I'm not qualified to teach school. I had taught a few Sunday School classes, and had taken a couple of education courses at NT. You need a teaching certificate for this, don't you? This is where divine intervention and the blessed people you know enter the equation.

I had an interview with Irving Superintendent W.T. Haynes, who offered me a job on the spot (They must have been pretty hard up for teachers!), and as he searched my college transcript to find something I might be qualified for, I got a very pleasant and unexpected surprise. It turns out that just by happenstance, I had taken twelve hours of education courses which qualified me for a "Lifetime Provisional Elementary Teaching Certificate." I could not believe it! In those earlier times before more rigorous academic qualifications for teaching certificates, twelve hours of education, with no student teaching, gave me this piece of paper which I would be able to use for the rest of my public school teaching career in Texas. And why did I take those twelve hours of education? Primarily because the Head of Elementary Education at NT was a distinguished professor named James Dougherty who was also a Sig Ep Alum and whose sons, James and Charles, were classmates from DHS and became my fellow Sig Eps. Dr. Dougherty would later be the major professor on my Ph.D. program.

25.

On the Tuesday after Labor Day, 1957, I began my teaching career at Crockett Junior High in Irving, teaching seventh and eighth grade science, eighth grade history and ninth grade world history. That's a mouthful, *no es*? To say I was not qualified to teach seventh and eighth grade science is an understatement! I had had exactly six hours of required biology and not another science course as an undergraduate. Needless to say, I struggled, staying a chapter ahead of the kids and having as many foaming, smelly science experiments as I could get away with. Oh, yes, I was also taking three night law school classes, nine hours, at SMU.

By Thanksgiving I was beyond exhausted and needed a break. The law school classes were harder than anything I had ever studied; so much reading of cases, writing case studies, but no tests. There would be only one, the final, and all would depend on how well I did on that exam. Very quickly, I found out I had never really learned to study, so learn I did, burning the midnight oil after class five nights a week, spending Saturdays and Sunday afternoons in the SMU Law Library, getting by on four or five hours sleep each night. Not much time for a social life.

The break I needed came in a very unexpected and surprising way. Coming up was a much needed four-day Thanksgiving Holiday, but my big break came in the form of a phone call on the Wednesday afternoon just before we got out of school for the holiday. Superintendent Haynes called the school office, leaving a message for me to come to his office when school was out. When the school secretary delivered the message in person, I got pretty nervous. What had I done? Was I allowing my law school classes interfere with doing my teaching job? By the time I got to the Administrative Offices that afternoon I was thinking the worst.

There was no need to worry. Mr. Haynes said he thought he had something for me that matched my undergraduate preparation. Was I interested? You bet I was, tell me more. Well, there was a lot to tell, and not much of it was good.

It seems the man who was supposed to be teaching American Government (Civics) at Irving High

School had not shown up for work in over six weeks, claiming he was too ill to work. These four classes of Junior and Senior students had not had a regular teacher since September, and had a total of five different substitute teachers since then.

"It won't be easy, Jim, but I'll bet you can do it," Mr. Haynes said, then added, "It'll sure help us out."

How could I refuse?   Teaching American Government in High School is exactly what I would have chosen to teach if given the choice when school began in September. Tough or not, I would give it a shot. The task of starting a new teaching assignment in the middle of the school year was daunting, but not having to teach science to seventh and eighth graders was consolation enough.

My transfer to Irving High began immediately on the Monday after the Thanksgiving Holiday, and it was not easy.

I have often reflected on this first year of teaching, and particularly on my time at IHS. Those three weeks between Thanksgiving and Christmas were brutal. Many of the kids thought I was just another sub they could run off, and they tried pretty much everything they could think of, but it didn't work.

Why? Probably a combination of things: I knew and loved the subject area I was teaching and was excited about teaching it, and I had tried or knew about virtually all the stunts the kids used on me to rattle my cage. Remember, I was just barely 21, not that far removed from high school hi-jinks myself. Too green and inexperienced to be afraid, I plunged ahead, and as 1958 began, things began to get better. By Easter things were going very well: The Senior Class asked me to be one of their sponsors, and by the time the end of the school year rolled around I was sorry to say "Goodbye."

They were a great bunch of kids, and this as much as anything else was probably the reason I made it through my first year of teaching relatively sane and unscarred. After checking me out pretty good, they settled in for the rest of the school year. During our time together those students learned a lot about our government and how it works. And me? I learned a lot more than they did—about how important it is to love what you teach, who you teach, and to show it every day. More about this later.

The experience of teaching about our political system and how it works was a segue' to a major change in my life, though I didn't know it at the time. The end of the school year at Irving High School also marked the end of my first year of law school at SMU. Only three more to go if I continued on at night. Whoopie!

Struggling through a couple of classes during the summer, I was worn out and needed a break. Was law school really for me? I liked the study of law, but wasn't really sure I wanted to be an attorney. Studying day and night, I never seemed to have enough time to learn all I needed to learn—the highest grade I made in any class was an 86.

About the time school was out at the end of May, I had gotten my induction notice for the Army. I had been deferred while in college, so I flinched when I opened the letter from Uncle Sam, knowing what was coming up. A few weeks later I appeared for my Army physical, along with several dozen other guys, at the induction center in Dallas. Almost through the seemingly endless process, the doctor who was checking my respiration and lungs asked me to move over to another spot, where he checked me out even more thoroughly, then asked if I had allergies or asthma. Having had hay fever since high school, I said, "Yes." He then handed me a form and said I should have my family doctor in Denton check me out, said it sounded like I had asthma.

The next week I went to see Dr. Adami, who had been my family physician for years, for another exam. He checked me out, we talked for a while, then he looked at the form and said, "Jimmy, you really don't want to go into the Army, do you?"

"I do not," I said emphatically.

I had been in the Air Force ROTC at North Texas for the first two years, then dropped out when I knew I was going to graduate in three years. Those two years of

Rotsie military training had been enough for me.

"Well," Dr. Adami said, "you won't have to go. You have developed psychosomatic asthma, probably brought on by your rigorous year of teaching and law school."

4-F. It was as simple as that, but really not that simple since I had noticed some wheezing and shortness of breath on occasion. Maybe this hard year had a positive outcome after all, but it came at a price—I have had bouts with asthma off and on for years, particularly during stressful times.

As I considered my options during the summer of 1958, I decided to contact my undergrad advisor at UNT for advice. Dr. Sam McAlister was Head of the Political Science/Government Department and had been involved in local and state politics for some time. As we discussed some of the career choices open to me, out of the blue he asked if I was interested in working in Washington, D.C. for our Congressman, Frank Ikard. The Congressman and he were old friends, former college roommates, and communicated frequently. At first I was stunned by the question, and moments later got excited by the possibilities. The thought of living and working in D.C. had never crossed my mind, and for a U.S. Congressman, WOW!

"Yes, I would," I stammered, so he picked up the phone on the spot and called Congressman Ikard. Three weeks later I had packed my stuff in my 1950 Mercury and was headed northeast toward Washington, D.C. and a brand new life.

Driving toward that first sunrise was both scary and exciting. I really did not know what I would be doing, just that I had a political patronage job arranged by the Congressman, and could transfer my SMU Law School credits to George Washington University Law School and enroll for the fall term. I could stay for a week or two at the Sig Ep fraternity house on the GWU campus until the fall term began. After that I would need another place to live.

I have been amazed at the good fortune of meeting people who come along at just the right time in my life, a repeated confirmation of a long-held belief that it's not *what* you know, but *who* you know that often makes the difference—nothing in life is more important than relationships. The next example on this score was showing up at Congressman Ikard's office my first day in D.C., meeting his Administrative Assistant, Jim Boren, who told me of the job possibilities a political patronage guy like me could have.

"I'll bet you'd rather work for Senator Yarbrough than Congressman Ikard, wouldn't you?"

"Yeah," I said hesitantly, hoping it wasn't a trick question.

"Well," Boren said, "there are more jobs and more clout with the Senator, and I'm moving over to be his Administrative Assistant in a couple of days. So come on over and we'll have something that pays better and is more interesting over on the Senate side."

So that's how, three days after arriving in D.C., I went to work as a political leach for Senator Ralph Yarbrough from Texas, a man who I knew almost nothing about, but who would soon become one of my all-time heroes. More about the Senator later.

Working and living in Washington, D.C. was a mind-blower at first. Hard to believe I was there, working in a place I had studied about, taught about, but never seen; and working for a United States Senator no less. Truth be told, the work was for someone pretty far down the status ladder, but did I care? Peon or not, it was immensely interesting just being in the Senate Office Building, the Capitol, and riding the streetcar to classes past the White House on a daily basis.

And the people! Fairly frequently, I saw Lyndon Johnson, Richard Nixon, Estes Kefauver (Democratic VP nominee in '56), Chief Justice Earl Warren, Speaker of the House Sam Rayburn (also a Texan and LBJ's mentor), and many others whose notoriety has since faded into history. And on only a couple of occasions, Jack Kennedy, who was already running for president, and frequently absent campaigning. Considered by most of his fellow senators to be a lightweight since he was only a first-term freshman senator, but he may have been the first modern-day stealth candidate, 'cause he sure snuck up on 'em. Kennedy was a non-entity with little clout when I was there in '58–'59, known as the "ghost senator," but he had Daddy Joe's money and political influence.

Memorable moments: There were several. A biggy was meeting Harry Truman. When he was Vice President he became a good friend of Texan Sam Rayburn, for many years the powerful Speaker of the House. They were weekly poker-playing buddies, and when Rayburn retired in early 1959, Truman came to a luncheon at the Capitol for the Texas delegation hosted by Texas Congressman Jack Brooks from Houston (who was later defeated by Bush 41). All the Texas delegation in Congress attended, and so did a number of their staff. Well, we didn't have a seat at the luncheon, but we kinda hung around the edges. We were standing outside the room where the food was being served when Truman came in and started shaking hands and greeting people. He shook my hand as I introduced myself. At the end of the luncheon as we were standing around as the guests left, Truman came out, shook my hand and said, "Jimmy, it was nice to meet you." I was thunderstruck—President Truman remembered my name!

Another memorable moment in early 1959 was seeing Fidel Castro and Che' Guevarra in their army fatigues hop out of a just-arrived jeep caravan (looked like the Keystone Cops to me) and stride up the Senate Chamber steps to meet with the Senate Foreign Relations Committee. A few months earlier Castro and his guerilla army had defeated the Cuban dictator Samosa, and he was being courted by all the international community as a hero of the Cuban people. At that time no one knew of his communist leanings, but we found out pretty soon, and we all know what long-term effects his choices have had on the world up to this very day. The chaos depicted in the Havana segment of *Godfather II* showing the downfall of Samosa is probably fairly realistic.

Early one morning, a couple of months after arriving in D.C., I was walking around the East Front Capitol grounds in my police garb (congress was recessed for something, perhaps Armistice Day). It was a beautiful, crisp fall day, the leaves were turning and drifting lazily down, the turf littered with their reds and golds. I had just seen Chief Justice Earl Warren walking across the grounds past the FDR Carillon to the Supreme Court, just across the way from the Capitol, something he did every day when the Court was in session.

I was pretty impressed by this sighting, and standing there in awe I looked as a Cadillac convertible, top down, whizzed around the drive in front of me and quickly pulled into a "No Parking" slot. The driver, a bushy-haired young man, not much older than me, hopped out, grabbed a worn leather briefcase and quickly strode away. He looked vaguely familiar, and moving closer I realized it was Robert Kennedy, then the chief counsel for the Kefauver Anti-Racketeering Committee. I only recognized him because I had seen him on TV questioning Jimmy Hoffa during the highly-publicized hearings investigating organized crime. Having no idea how famous and inspiring a figure he would become, at the time I was frankly more impressed with seeing Earl Warren walking to work. I mean, what law student wouldn't be impressed seeing the chief judge of the land strolling to work in the morning? As I walked by Bobby's Caddy I noticed the backseat littered with parking tickets. Wonder if he ever paid them?

When Congress was in session I could often be found lugging stacks of printed material around for the Senator, or waiting in the Senate Cloak Room or outside the Senate Chamber to give him or his senior staff stuff. The Senate convened at twelve-noon each day, and usually you could tell when the Vice President was coming to preside because he was always preceded by a Secret Service agent who looked like Nixon's double. The double was the same size as Tricky Dicky and wore the same color suit.

And sure enough, about ten or fifteen yards behind, the real guy walked up. I saw Nixon a number of times as he arrived to preside over the Senate and I never saw him smile or stop to speak to anyone. He was already practicing his now famous scowl.

What job did I have that gave this kind of personal view of these people and events? There were two, really, and whichever one I was working depended on whether Congress was in session. In session I worked as a gofer and administrative aide out of Senator Yarbrough's office, running errands, showing visitors around the Capitol, carrying printed materials (tons of it) to meeting rooms and other senate offices. When Congress was not in session nearly all the members went back home, and there was much less to do, so I donned the uniform of a Capitol policeman and patrolled around on the Senate side of the Capitol, or stationed outside the Senate Gallery, sat at an ornate desk and studied. Was I a real cop? No, but I played one in D.C.

During an eight-hour work day, I was often able to study three or four hours, sometimes in the Senate Law Library, and elegant and totally resourced hideaway. Even though I worked six days a week it was a pretty cushy job, one that gave me a window into some of the inner workings of the Senate, and not infrequently a look at foibles and human frailties of elected officials. Estes Kefauver, for example, the Democratic Vice-Presidential candidate in '56, a florid-faced alcoholic who kept a Dixie cup full of bourbon covered by a napkin on the desk outside the Senate Chamber; or LBJ, then the powerful Senate Majority Leader, who went frequently into one of the many hidden offices in the bowels of the Capitol with his beautiful Administrative Assistant, Mary Margaret Murphy (about whom I and other staffers had some impure thoughts), emerging later rearranging his tie and shooting the cuffs of his shirt sleeves. Probably just resting after a long day at the office.

There were also examples of courtesy and selflessness. My respect and admiration for Senator Yarbrough took a leap one day as he made his way down the hallway of the Senate Office Building to one of the endless committee meetings, me trailing behind carrying a sizeable sheaf of papers. He stopped to speak to a janitor working in the hallway, asked his how his daughter's operation had gone, spoke quietly with him for a moment, then pulled out his wallet, handed the black man a $20 bill, touched his shoulder, and walked away. Not sure anyone but me saw that simple act of kindness and generosity, but it said a lot to me about the character of this soft-spoken man, a former county judge from the Rio Grande Valley. I was proud to work for him.

A word about political patronage jobs, the kind of job I had. Each member of Congress was allocated a certain number of these patronage jobs, mostly for persons who worked in their offices, on their committee staffs, or other related congressional positions. These jobs were allocated on the basis of length of seniority and political party currently in power. Senator Yarbrough, as the junior senator from Texas, had a number of patronage jobs, and LBJ, the senior senator and Majority Leader of the Senate, had many more.

One of my Sig Ep fraternity brothers, Tommy Wallace, was a staff member of the Senate Preparedness Sub-Committee (of the Armed Services Committee) which Johnson chaired, and also worked in Johnson's senate office during congressional recesses, sometimes at his Austin senatorial office. Tommy's job had way more clout than mine, and he came by it deservedly—he had been ROTC Colonel of the Corps at UNT when I was a freshman, had just spent three years as an Air Force Officer, and when they wouldn't let him fly anymore, mustered out early to take this job. We palled around some, went on a couple of double dates with rich girls from Greenbriar College near Lynchburg, Virginia, a ritzy girl's school where a lot of the girls had their own horses, and on several early Saturday mornings when Congress was not in session, spent a couple of hours raising and lowering U.S. flags over the Capitol Building. Hey, lots of influential visitors wanted a U.S. flag that had flown over the Capitol. Anything for a prominent patron, right? Did I forget to mention that it was an interesting year?

Tommy and I would regularly put our heads together, scheming over some get-rich-quick idea. He wanted to be rich and I didn't think it was such a bad idea. We thought we had a sure-fire one when Alaska became the 49th state and one of our senate staff buddies, an Eskimo working for Delegate (later Senator) Groening told us we could get a tiny island (about 100 acres) in Southeast Alaska only for the cost of filing for it. He said he would help us get it.

Why this tiny island? Well, after researching it and several others as well, we determined there were no natural predators on the island, that eggs were selling for a buck a piece in Alaska, so why not start a chicken farm on the island and get rich selling eggs. We had a few other hair-brained schemes like this, and soon learned that Native Alaskans had prior claim to the island, so we moved on. Tommy did get rich, and he did so the easy way—he married the rich girl he was dating at Greenbriar, the daughter of a prominent West Texas sheep rancher. The last time I heard from him, a few years later, he was on the San Angelo town council, where his wife was from.

A few weeks after arriving in D.C. I went to a young people's social event at my new church and met a lovely young woman who would soon become my wife. Jean Massey's beauty and charm ensnared me, and after a whirlwind romance we were married in January, 1959. Soon after we were married, Jean and I drove to West Virginia so I could meet her family. They lived in the small town of Stickney, about 50 miles from Charleston. Her father, Finley, was an electrician in a coal mine, and at the time we visited them, was the only man in that small town of 600 who had a job.

Jean's family had been coal miners for several generations. Her grandfather, a tall, handsome man with a shock of snow white hair, had gone into the mines at age twelve and worked for 53 years, coming out of the mines at the mandatory retirement age of 65.

Finley Massey was a kind and generous man who had led a varied and interesting life. He was now lay minister in a Presbyterian Church, where Jean had been the church pianist, but at a younger age had made moonshine and home brew. The story is told that Finley got religion when the family was hosting the preacher for Sunday Dinner. As the family was seated and ready to eat, they heard popping sounds coming from the basement. A few days earlier Finley had made a batch of home brew but the concoction was not exactly right—it began noisily blowing the tops off of the bottles in the middle of the preacher's noontime prayer. He came to Jesus that very day.

When I expressed an interest in the coal mining industry Finley was happy to explain the process being used at that time, and asked if I would like to spend an eight-hour shift with him in the mine. "Sure would," said I, so a day later went with Finley to his mining operation, traveling on the four-foot-tall coal train with other miners on his shift for what seemed like miles back into the depths of the mountain. The way coal was extracted from this mine was to dig back into the coal deposits as far as the vein of coal went, then begin extracting coal from the seam, sometimes leaving large caverns, none seemed taller than six to eight feet, but often hundreds of feet across. In order to prevent the mountain from caving in after the coal was removed, solid timbers were placed at intervals in the now empty caverns to hold the roof up. As I walked through some of these caverns with timbers supporting the roof, I could hear timbers cracking from the tremendous pressure of the mountain. Talk about a scary feeling! That eight hour shift spent in the mine was an unforgettable experience.

About this same time I decided Law School wasn't for me. I liked the study of law, but was not sure about the practice of law. I had been hooked by that first year of teaching, and wanted to return to Texas to teach again, so we did.

But I was hooked on Washington and loved living there. I was to return again to live there in 1975, and returned dozens of times since then on Head Start and other early childhood-related business.

In addition to meeting Jean at the 16th and Decatur Street Church of Christ, I also met two guys who became my roommates. We rented a large, rambling upstairs apartment at 123 Independence Avenue, S.E., just across the street from the Library of Congress and Capitol grounds. What a great location! The building holding our apartment has long been demolished as the Feds built more and more office buildings to house congressional offices, but in 1958 it was part of a vibrant neighborhood with a full complement of businesses and living spaces. On the street level below our apartment was a White Castle (where you could get ten mini-burgers for a dollar!), a liquor store, a dry cleaners, and down on the corner a neighborhood bar and grill where Lowell, one of my roommates, played piano for a couple of hours three or four nights a week for his meals—he was also song leader at church, had a beautiful voice and was a great musician. My other roommate, David, was a student at Georgetown University and worked for Congressman John Jarmon of Oklahoma.

I parked my Mercury on the Capitol Grounds a block away and walked to work each morning. After work I hopped on the trolley across the street from our apartment and rode it all the way to law classes at GWU, passing the White House going and coming. How cool is that!

If D.C. sounds a bit different then than it is now, it *was* different, very different. The politics were kinder, more collegial and open to compromise, far less acerbic or divisive. I can only speak about the Senate since that's the side I worked on, but there were also many opportunities to know what was going on in the House, and I never saw the kind of disrespect or outright hatred I see on the news from Washington these days. It makes me very sad and fearful that our democracy is devolving into an oligarchy and a plutocracy controlled by the wealthiest Americans. What kind of country will our grandchildren inherit?

27.

I am one of the lucky ones, whose best childhood memories all contain birdsong and trees. We had no idea we were living at the edge of an epoch, tasting the remains of a great, newly plowed continent . . .

Barbara Kingsolver, *Last Stand: America's Virgin Lands.*

Each fall around Thanksgiving, we eagerly await the return of Golden and Bald Eagle pairs to our stretch of the Animas River where they nest and hatch chicks among the crags of rocky mesas which define our eastern horizon. The eagles hatched several weeks ago have begun their flight but are still pretty young to fly very far, but what do I know about how far a young Bald or Golden Eagle can fly in a day or a week? Each observation of one of these majestic raptors we count as a blessing, and we are blessed most days.

Now, as April days lengthen, we have looked in vain for a week; maybe they've headed north to their summer haunts in Canada or Alaska. I miss them already, these majestic birds we have come to love in a possessive way. They have become ours, and we look frequently for them. They have been so plentiful this year—we're spoiled by an abundance of eagles.

Five years ago, during our first November in this secluded perch above the Animas River here on the northwestern edge of New Mexico, Susan and I were delighted, but not surprised to see a Bald Eagle sitting in the large cottonwood tree across the river from our house. We had been told they would be here; the former owner had teased us with this tidbit soon after we arrived to look at the place. But seeing one so close, our very own, was thrilling. This eagle and its mate have been coming back each year now, and always in late winter/early spring an eaglet kid also appears. Sometimes both have sat in the same old cottonwood across the river, and once, the whole family—mom, dad, and the kid—were there one morning as the sun came over the eastern mesa. What a treat!

Three years ago a pair of Goldens appeared, with a kid in the spring, and this eagle season we have seen both Bald and Golden Eagles almost every day. Two weeks ago, a front page article in the

Farmington Daily Times featured a woman living a couple of miles south of us who was quoted as counting 28 eagles around her place in a single day. We think she was exaggerating; probably confused a bunch of buzzards with eagles. There are always buzzards in the spring, summer and fall skies; not so many during winter. That's the eagles' time.

The lady's tale aside, there have been lots of eagles this year. One day about noontime three weeks ago, the Austin Workmans were visiting and I was returning home from a shopping trip. As I came over the rise onto our property three Golden Eagles were circling above our house, and two or three hundred feet above them, two Bald Eagles circled. Susan, Andrew, Anna and Max were outside but unaware of this raptor omen circling above them. It was a blessed day.

But now they're gone, north to hunt along some river in Montana, British Columbia or Alaska. The angst over their departure is tempered by the anticipated arrival of another set of feathered friends—tiny ones—hummingbirds, usually around the first of May. And sure enough, today as we sip morning coffee and read the Saturday paper I look out to see a miniature scout outside a riverside window, looking for a sugary fix from absent feeders. Wheeling to glare in at us, his demanding stare prompts a scurry to get the hummingbird feeders out of storage and prepare sugar water to fill them; spring really is here.

28.

Sin agua no hay vida
Without water there is no life

Here in the spring of 2003 we are in the midst of the driest year since moving to New Mexico. Since November there has been less than one inch of precipitation. It is very dry, even in this high desert mesa country which averages less than ten inches per year, in the third year of a drought that may get serious before the end of summer. Hydrologists report very low snow pack in the mountains, foretelling lower spring runoffs. Farmers are worried that irrigation water may run out before August. Forest and range fires have already started this year, and without a significant (and unlikely) amount of rain or snow in the high country, this could be the worst fire season in many years. Most experts are saying it is already too late for spring snow to do any good.

Before moving to this rural spot, it was easy to imagine the Farmington municipal infrastructure keeping a buffer zone around our daily needs; we

~ 237 ~

could always turn on the faucet outside to water our small garden of tomatoes, peppers and broccoli. Even the every-other-day water rationing initiated on two occasions was not a bother. But of course that imaginary buffer zone was just that—not real. Here in the desert southwest we are never far from water scarcity. Something I read a couple of years ago now seems very prophetic: *The major currency of the 20th century was energy; the currency of the 21st century will be water, particularly in the west.*

In truth I've always paid attention to the weather—the country boy in me keeping a tiller-of-the-soil's eye out for rain, snow, a storm cloud, a high wind—whatever affects the crops. For many years, like all who farm or garden, I've fretted about water, or the lack of it, in the Southwest. This is the first year it has become a major concern. More than a third of the "hardy" and "needs little water" trees, shrubs and bushes I've planted the last three years died during this past cold, dry winter. I am reminded of the seven year drought we experienced in Texas in the 1950s. This one seems worse.

This is the year we hoped to become self-sufficient. When we moved here in the spring of

1997, we said we would give ourselves five years to develop our organic vegetable garden and fruit orchard to the point we could live year round on the summer and fall harvest. We have done pretty well, filling two freezers with frozen green beans, green chilies, corn, homemade salsa and other vegetables. The pantry is loaded with canned apples and applesauce, peaches, apricots, tomatoes and a variety of jams. We rarely buy vegetables at Safeway; it's been years since I've bought a tomato. This summer will be number five, and we hope to grow enough surplus organic veggies to sell at the local farmer's market or donate to the local food bank. Food-wise, we have done pretty good, but self-sufficiency is more than growing what we eat.

The other part of the independent life is converting our energy dependence from grid-provided power to renewable energy sources: wind turbine, photovoltaic and a solar hot water system. We've moved in that direction, but energy independence is still a few years away. Last fall I began taking classes in renewable energy at San Juan College and now feel confident that, with some professional help, I can do much of the work converting to renewable energy.

My desire for a wind turbine has diminished somewhat after we had a pro come out to do a property assessment, with the result that generating electricity from wind energy here may not be very cost effective. Bummer.

Energy from the sun we have in abundance—over 300 days of sunshine each year. It's water that's iffy, and this summer is looking worse than most.

A pause in writing this to wander to the river side of the house to peer east, out the wall of glass toward the greening alfalfa orbs across the river on the Kysar Ranch, embroidered on a narrow collar of land between the river and the abrupt mesa wall thrusting into a cobalt sky. Even this digression to stare at the eye-catching vista speaks of this dry season: The river, usually rising and opaque with snow melt by now, is running clear and low with almost no high country runoff yet.

A few days later I am awakened during the night by the sound of rain on the roof, a rare and welcome sound. My hopes are short-lived; after a few minutes the wet tapping slows, stops. Just a brief shower, a teaser, hardly enough to settle the dust. Intermittent showers for a while, then as the sun is an hour old in the east, it breaks out. In the solar-impaired Pacific Northwest, weatherpersons say days like this will have "sun breaks." Here we call them "partly cloudy," just another day in our corner of paradise.

29.

Kenyan Sunset

<u>**Late October, 2013**</u>

Happy, smiling faces of uniformed school children beam at us, waving a greeting as we pass by on roadways near schools beginning or ending their school day. During our trek around Kenya we have seen many such smiles and waves; are told that passing tourists sometimes toss treats to them, but I choose to believe the smiles and waves are mostly due to the eager enthusiasm with which most children greet life.

And it is quite a life here in this diverse, now-dusty, strife-torn country of which Disney, PBS and the Discovery Channel have only given us peeks and sniffs, the real McCoy is a whole other thing: The majestic beauty of Mt. Kenya; traveling to and through the Masai Mara where countless thousands of animals roam and migrate, hunter and hunted everywhere; bright red wraps of tall, slender Masai warriors around their village; the incredible, unobstructed view from our hilltop perch at the Masai Mara Lodge looking south, east and west for 60+ miles to the horizon, seeing an endless array of animals unique to this part of the world.

But perhaps most of all the sense of how blessed and fortunate we are to see all this before it vanishes, as it slowly is here and other parts of Africa. The Masai migrated here from Egypt in 1,500 A.D. What this country must have been like back then! In my younger days I sometimes fantasized about being an explorer in Africa two hundred years ago—perhaps too much Stanley and Livingston.   That dream trip finally came true.

On our last trek in from a day-long journey of looking for and finally getting some rare close-ups of a cheetah and some lions, we marvel at the changing golden to crimson, now magenta sunset view of distant acacias silhouetted across the western horizon, a picture-book ending to our Kenyan adventure.

Afrika
Afrika Afrika
Afrika

So now we come to the end of our journey through those early years, coming full circle back where we started in this corner of New Mexico. Ten years later, similar weather patterns, but not the same arid, end-of-summer water deficits: During the past two weeks we have had an unusually wet late-summer time, too late to do the about-finished garden much good, but always welcome in this moisture-deficient country. This one-time abundance of rain helps wash away some of those dry-times memories.

Maw Maw and Mom would be proud of this Gage family's continued reliance on the products of the soil, of our garden. The freezers and pantry are full of our summer harvest bounty. Remembering those long-ago times with my grandmother as I reveled in her gentle, intimate presence, preparing her harvest for later enjoyment, I am happy to report we are following in your footsteps, Maw Maw. As the writer in Ecclesiastes says, one generation passes

away, and another generation comes; but the earth
abides forever.

www.ingramcontent.com/pod-product-compliance
Lightning Source LLC
Chambersburg PA
CBHW071601030726
47593CB00001BA/264